2017 上半年
First Half of 2017

中国国际收支报告
China's Balance of Payments Report

国家外汇管理局国际收支分析小组
BOP Analysis Group
State Administration of Foreign Exchange

中国金融出版社
China Financial Publishing House

责任编辑：张翠华
责任校对：孙　蕊
责任印制：程　颖

图书在版编目（CIP）数据

2017 上半年中国国际收支报告 (2017 Shangbannian Zhongguo Guoji Shouzhi
Baogao)/ 国家外汇管理局国际收支分析小组编 . —北京：中国金融出版社，2018.1
　ISBN 978-7-5049-9409-7

　Ⅰ . ① 2… 　Ⅱ . ①国 … 　Ⅲ . ①国际收支—研究报告—中国—2017
Ⅳ . ① F812.4

　中国版本图书馆 CIP 数据核字（2018）第 016739 号

出版
发行　**中国金融出版社**

社址　　北京市丰台区益泽路 2 号
市场开发部　　（010）63266347，63805472，63439533　（传真）
网上书店　http://www.chinafph.com　（010）63286832，63365686　（传真）
读者服务部　　（010）66070833，62568380
邮编　　100071
经销　　新华书店
印刷　　天津银博印刷集团有限公司
尺寸　　210 毫米 ×285 毫米
印张　　11.75
字数　　216 千
版次　　2018 年 1 月第 1 版
印次　　2018 年 1 月第 1 次印刷
印数　　1–2000
定价　　80.00 元
ISBN　978-7-5049-9409-7
如出现印装错误本社负责调换　联系电话：（010）63263947

国家外汇管理局
国际收支分析小组人员名单

组　　　长：潘功胜
副 组 长：杨国中　郑　薇　张　新　陆　磊　张生会
审　　　稿：孙天琦　刘　斌　郭　松　徐卫刚　崔汉忠
统　　　稿：王春英　周　济　贾　宁　韩　健　赵玉超
执　　　笔：
第一部分：李　萌　王架浩　张青青
第二部分：陈　丰　马玉娟　常国栋　胡　红　高　畅
第三部分：杨　灿
第四部分：梁　艳　程娅婕
第五部分：管恩杰
专　　　栏：姜　骥　赵玉超　鲁峰华　王国建　李玲青　贺　萌　胡蓝引

附录整理：王架浩

英文翻译：周海文　王　亮　胡　红　杨　灿
英文审校：Nancy Hearst（美国哈佛大学费正清东亚研究中心）

Contributors to this Report

Head
Pan Gongsheng

Deputy Head
Yang Guozhong   Zheng Wei   Zhang Xin   Lu Lei   Zhang Shenghui

Readers
Sun Tianqi   Liu Bin   Guo Song   Xu Weigang   Cui Hanzhong

Editors
Wang Chunying   Zhou Ji   Jia Ning   Han Jian   Zhao Yuchao

Authors
Part One: Li Meng   Wang Jiahao   Zhang Qingqing
Part Two: Chen Feng   Ma Yujuan   Chang Guodong   Hu Hong   Gao Chang
Part Three: Yang Can
Part Four: Liang Yan   Cheng Yajie
Part Five: Guan Enjie
Boxes: Jiang Ji   Zhao Yuchao   Lu Fenghua   Wang Guojian   Li Lingqing
       He Meng   Hu Lanyin

Appendix: Wang Jiahao

Translators: Zhou Haiwen   Wang Liang   Hu Hong   Yang Can

Proofreader: Nancy Hearst (Fairbank Center for East Asian Research,
             Harvard University)

内容摘要

2017 年上半年，全球经济继续平稳复苏，主要经济体货币政策仍有分化，国际金融市场波动性下降；我国经济稳中向好态势更趋明显，金融市场运行保持平稳，人民币对美元汇率稳中有升。

2017 年上半年，我国国际收支呈现基本平衡，经常账户、非储备性质的金融账户重现"双顺差"，外汇储备稳步回升。首先，经常账户持续顺差，上半年为 693 亿美元，与 GDP 之比为 1.2%，仍处于合理区间。其中，货物贸易差额与 GDP 之比为 3.9%，服务贸易差额与 GDP 之比为 -2.4%。其次，跨境资本流动形势回稳向好，非储备性质的金融账户重现顺差，上半年为 679 亿美元，2016 年同期为逆差 1 787 亿美元。其中，境内主体对外投资更加理性有序，上半年直接投资、证券投资、其他投资等对外资产累计净增加 1 342 亿美元，同比少增 45%；境外主体来华各类投资较快回升，上半年累计净流入 2 021 亿美元，同比上升 2.2 倍。截至 2017 年 6 月末，我国外汇储备余额为 30 568 亿美元，较 2016 年末上升 463 亿美元。

2017 年下半年，预计我国经常账户将维持较合理的顺差规模，跨境资本流动保持总体稳定。未来在国内经济企稳向好、对外开放逐步加深、市场预期进一步趋稳的情况下，我国国际收支平衡的基础将更加稳固。外汇管理部门将紧紧围绕服务实体经济、防控金融风险、深化金融改革三项任务开展工作，继续坚持改革开放，提升贸易和投资便利化水平，积极防范跨境资本流动风险，维护外汇市场健康稳定发展。

Abstract

During the first half of 2017, the global economy recovered steadily, although the monetary policies of the major economies were diversified and volatility in the international financial market declined. The Chinese economy registered stable performance, with clearly good momentum for growth. The financial market remained stable and the RMB exchange rate against the USD steadily appreciated.

During the first half of the year, China's international balance of payments maintained a general equilibrium, with both the current account and the non-reserve financial account reappearing with a "dual surplus." There was an increase in foreign reserves. First, the current account maintained a surplus of USD 69.3 billion, and the ratio of the surplus to GDP was a reasonable 1.2 percent. In particular, the ratio of the balance of trade in goods to GDP was 3.9 percent and the ratio of trade in services to GDP was-2.4 percent. Second, cross-border capital flows recorded a steady rise. A surplus of USD 67.9 million reappeared in the non-reserve financial account, whereas in the first half of 2016 it had recorded a deficit of USD 178.7 billion. In particular, the external assets of direct investments, portfolio investments, and other investments recorded a net increase of USD 134.2 billion, down by 45 percent year on year and indicating that overseas investments by domestic entities were becoming more rational. Inward investments by foreign entities were recovering rapidly, with a net inflow of USD 202.1 billion during the first half of the year, up by 2.2 times year on year. By the end of June 2017, China's outstanding foreign reserves totaled USD 3056.8 billion, up by USD 46.3 billion from the end of 2016.

During the second half of 2017, the current account is expected to maintain a reasonable surplus and cross-border capital flows will remain stable. With such stabilization and improvements in the domestic economy, the intensification of the opening-up and the stabilized market expectations, the foundation for China's BOP equilibrium will solidify. The SAFE will assume responsibility for the three major tasks of serving the real economy, guarding against financial risks, and intensifying the financial reforms. It will continue the opening-up process by facilitating trade and investment, actively guarding against the risks of cross-border capital flows, and promoting the healthy development of the foreign - exchange market.

目　录

专栏

图

表

Content

Boxes

Charts

Tables

一、国际收支概况

（一）国际收支运行环境

2017 年上半年，中国国际收支运行的内外部环境显著改善。虽然国际金融危机的深层次影响尚未消除，但全球经济延续平稳复苏态势，外部环境总体平稳，国内经济稳中向好态势更趋明显。

全球经济总体平稳复苏。上半年，全球经济继续呈现复苏趋势，国际货币基金组织（IMF）和经济合作与发展组织（OECD）先后上调 2017 年全球经济增速预期至 3.5%，但主要经济体的表现有所分化（见图 1-1）。美国经济复苏过程波折反复，经济增速波动回升，失业率保持低位运行，但推出财政刺激计划的进程不及预期削弱其经济增长预期。欧元区政治不确定性有所下降，经济基本面持续改善，但通胀动力仍不足。日本经济复苏动能积累，经济增长处于国际金融危机以来最好表现，通胀水平也趋向回升。新兴市场经济总体增长较快，但部分经济体仍面临调整与转型压力，特别是在全球总需求增长较缓慢、发达经济体货币政策可能转向的背景下，外需较弱与跨境资本波动等潜在风险依然存在。

发达与新兴市场经济体货币政策分化。主要发达经济体已经启动或者正在酝酿货币政策正常化进程。上半年，美联储两次提高联邦基金利率目标区间各 25 个基点

图 1-1

主要经济体经济增长率

图例：日本　欧元区　美国　巴西　印度

注：美国数据为季度环比折年率，其他经济体数据为季度同比。

数据来源：环亚经济数据库。

图 1-2

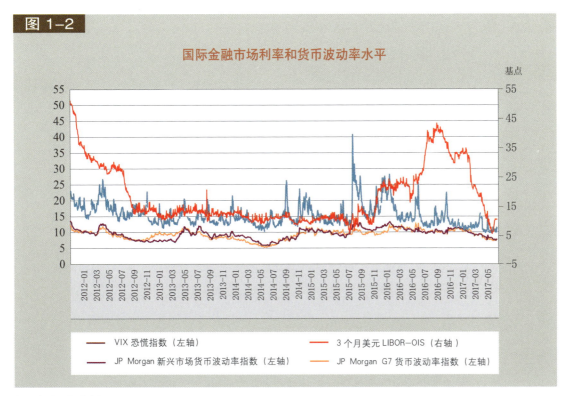

国际金融市场利率和货币波动率水平

数据来源：彭博资讯。

至 1%~1.25%，同时维持 2017 年再加息 1 次、2018 年加息 3 次的预期不变，并提出资产负债表正常化的计划。欧央行三次决定维持主要指标利率水平和资产购买计划不变，明确表示通缩风险已经消失。日本央行四次宣布维持原有负利率与资产购买规模不变，同时开始讨论退出量化宽松政策。新兴经济体货币政策有所分化，俄罗斯和巴西等部分经济体为促进经济增长进一步放松了货币政策，但墨西哥等一些经济体选择上调基准利率以应对汇率贬值、资本外流和通胀压力问题。

国际金融市场波动性下降。 受全球经济总体平稳复苏的支持，当前国际金融市场波动总体有所降低。2017 年上半年，美元走弱，欧元、英镑、日元对美元汇率大幅升值，美元指数下跌 6.4%；新兴市场货币涨跌互现，JP Morgan 新兴市场货币指数（EMCI）上涨 4.1%。2017 年上半年，市场避险情绪缓解，全球股市普遍上涨，大宗商品市场小幅上涨，VIX 恐慌指数下降 20.4%，美国道琼斯工业平均指数、欧元区斯托克 50 指数和明晟 MSCI 新兴市场股指分别上涨 8.0%、8.2% 和 17.2%，S&P GSCI 商品价格指数上涨 4.6%（见图 1-2 和图 1-3）。未来，主要经济体货币政策正常化、去全球化、贸易投资保护主义和地缘政治冲突等相关风险，仍可能对全球经济金融稳定带来挑战。

图 1-3

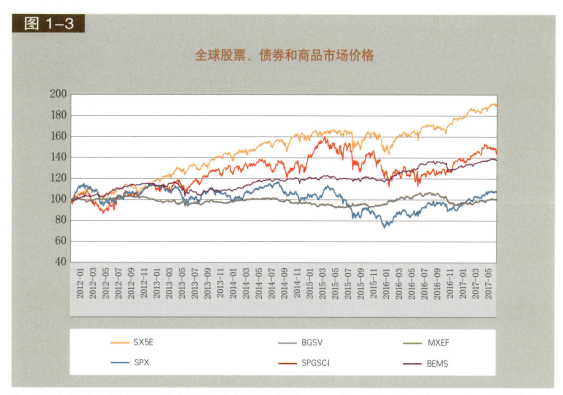

全球股票、债券和商品市场价格

图例：SX5E、BGSV、MXEF、SPX、SPGSCI、BEMS

注：BEMS 和 BGSV 分别为彭博新兴市场和发达国家主权债券指数，MXEF 为 MSCI 新兴市场股指，SPX 为美国标准普尔 500 股指，SX5E 为欧元区斯托克 50 股指，SPGSCI 为标准普尔 GSCI 商品价格指数，均以 2012 年初值为 100。

数据来源：彭博资讯。

图 1-4

我国季度 GDP 和月度 CPI 增长率

图例：季度 GDP 同比增长率（左轴）、月度 CPI 同比增长率（右轴）

数据来源：国家统计局。

国内经济稳中向好态势更趋明显。2017 年上半年，我国经济总体运行平稳，供给侧结构性改革深入推进，转型升级步伐加快，消费需求对经济增长的拉动作用保持强劲，投资和进出口保持稳定增长，经济发展的稳定性、协调性和可持续性增强。2017 年上半年，国内生产总值（GDP）达到 38.15 万亿元，同比增长 6.9%，居民消费价格指数（CPI）同比上涨 1.4%（见图 1-4），就业稳中向好，第三产业增加值占 GDP 的比重为 54.1%，最终消费支出对 GDP 增长的贡献率为 63.4%。但也必须看到，当前我国经济增长一定程度上受全球经济复苏背景下外需回暖的推动，经济内生增长动力有待进一步增强，结构性矛盾仍在稳步化解过程中。

专栏 1

美联储货币政策继续回归正常

2017 年 6 月，美联储货币政策会议决定将政策利率目标区间上调 25 个基点至 1%~1.25%，并宣布年内开始缩减资产负债表。声明附录明确，美联储将以减少到期证券本金再投资的方式渐进、可预测地缩表。起初每月缩表以 60 亿美元国债和 40 亿美元抵押支持证券（MBS）为上限，随后以每季度增加 60 亿美元国债和 40 亿美元 MBS 的节奏逐步扩大缩表上限规模，直至达到每月 300 亿美元国债和 200 亿美元 MBS 的上限规模。美联储主席耶伦表示，公布缩表计划是为了缓解市场紧张情绪，相信可以尽快实施，但若经济恶化也会适时调整。9 月，美联储货币政策会议维持政策利率水平不变，宣布在 10 月正式启动缩表进程，并预估年内再加息一次。

当前经济和市场环境有助于美联储维持全年加息 3 次并启动缩表的预定计划。美国已非常接近充分就业，4.3% 的失业率低于美联储估计的自然失业率（NAIRU），传统经济理论指示经济有过热风险，美联储对其加息步伐过慢的担忧上升。此外，当前利率仍较低，一旦发生危机，利率再次触及零下限的风险较高，尽早紧缩将有助于为未来创造更多政策空间。但是，仅加息无缩表不利于均衡收紧金融条件。加息抬升短端利率，而维持大规模资产负债表对中长端利率造成下行压力，扭曲利率曲线。因此，加息到一定程度后启动缩表是货币政策正常化的必然诉求。2016 年下半年以来，美国与全球经济数据普遍转好，今年法国大选等外围风险亦消退，为加息和缩表提供了适宜的时间窗口。

近期通胀数据疲弱，与美联储和市场预期背离，但美联储货币政策正常化的目标不会轻易改变。一是经济内生增长动能稳健。就业稳健增长、财富再创新高、信心持续高涨，预计居民消费将稳定增长。投资方面，油价处于健康区间、全球经济持续改善、前期美元升值拖累趋缓，工业产出与企业投资仍将温和增长。二是中期内通胀有望重回缓慢上升趋势。近期通胀走低，部分受到油价基数效应冲高回落、电信价格调整等短期因素扰动。随着经济持续复苏，通胀向美联储 2% 目标缓慢靠拢的趋势不改。三是金融条件持续放松。2016 年 12 月以来，美联储虽三次加息并公布缩表计划，但长端国债收益率和美元指数均震荡走低，股市也连创新高，为美联储进一步收紧货币政策留有空间，并增强美联储对资产泡沫的谨慎态度。

美联储收紧货币政策对新兴市场经济体的影响需持续关注。历史经验显示，若美联储加息速度超预期导致利率快速大幅上升，通常会导致新兴市场资本流出。我国作为全球最大的新兴市场经济体，不可避免也将面临一定的资本流动压力。但迄今为止，美联储货币政策正常化进程相对平稳，而且各国经济基本面仍是防范风险的关键。当前我国宏观经济稳中向好，经常账户仍处于盈余，外债规模可控，外汇储备规模稳定在 3 万亿美元左右，为应对外部环境变化提供了良好的缓冲。

（二）国际收支主要状况

2017 年上半年，我国国际收支重现经常账户、非储备性质的金融账户"双顺差"，两者顺差分别为 693 亿美元和 679 亿美元（见表 1–1）。

表 1–1　中国国际收支差额主要构成　　　　　　　　　　　　　　　　单位：亿美元

项　目	2011 年	2012 年	2013 年	2014 年	2015 年	2016 年	2016 年上半年	2017 年上半年
经常账户差额	1 361	2 154	1 482	2 360	3 042	1 964	1 103	693
与 GDP 之比	1.8%	2.5%	1.5%	2.3%	2.7%	1.8%	2.1%	1.2%
非储备性质的金融账户差额	2 600	−360	3 430	−514	−4 345	−4 170	−1 787	679
与 GDP 之比	3.4%	−0.4%	3.6%	−0.5%	−3.9%	−3.7%	−3.4%	1.2%

数据来源：国家外汇管理局，国家统计局。

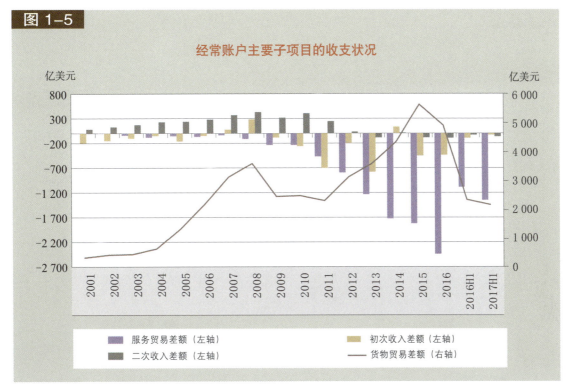

图 1-5

经常账户主要子项目的收支状况

亿美元 （左轴）　　　　　　　　　　　　　　　　　　　　　亿美元 （右轴）

图例：
- 服务贸易差额（左轴）
- 二次收入差额（左轴）
- 初次收入差额（左轴）
- 货物贸易差额（右轴）

数据来源：国家外汇管理局。

　　货物贸易持续顺差。 按国际收支统计口径①，2017 年上半年，我国货物贸易出口 10 269 亿美元，进口 8 126 亿美元，同比分别增长 12% 和 18%；顺差 2 144 亿美元，下降 8%（见图 1-5）。

　　服务贸易延续逆差。 2017 年上半年，服务贸易收入 1014 亿美元，同比增长 0.4%；支出 2 364 亿美元，增长 13%；逆差 1 351 亿美元，增长 24%。其中，运输项目逆差 262 亿美元，增长 26%；旅行项目逆差 1 159 亿美元，增长 19%（见图 1-5）。

　　初次收入②逆差收窄。 2017 年上半年，初次收入项下收入 1 250 亿美元，同比增长 15%；支出 1 284 亿美元，增长 9%；逆差 34 亿美元，下降 65%。其中，雇员报酬顺差 85 亿美元，同比下降 21%；投资收益逆差 122 亿美元，下降 41%（见图 1-5）。从投资收益看，我国对外投资的收益为 1 130 亿美元，增长 19%；外国来华投资的利润利息、股息红利等支出 1 252 亿美元，增长 9%。

---

　　① 本口径与海关口径的主要差异在于：一是国际收支中的货物只记录所有权发生了转移的货物（如一般贸易、进料加工贸易等贸易方式的货物），所有权未发生转移的货物（如来料加工或出料加工贸易）不纳入货物统计，而纳入服务贸易统计；二是计价方面，国际收支统计要求进出口货值均按离岸价格记录，海关出口货值为离岸价格，但进口货值为到岸价格，因此国际收支统计从海关进口货值中调出国际运保费支出，并纳入服务贸易统计；三是补充部分进出口退运等数据；四是补充了海关未统计的转手买卖下的货物净出口数据。

　　② 国际货币基金组织《国际收支和国际投资头寸手册》（第六版）将经常项下的"收益"名称改为"初次收入"，将"经常转移"名称改为"二次收入"。

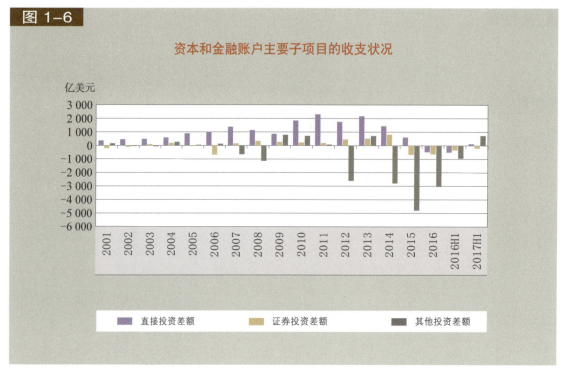

图 1-6

资本和金融账户主要子项目的收支状况

数据来源：国家外汇管理局。

二次收入逆差扩大。2017 年上半年，二次收入项下收入 147 亿美元，同比下降 9%；支出 213 亿美元，增长 9%；逆差 67 亿美元，增长 99%（见图 1-5）。

直接投资转为顺差。按国际收支统计口径，2017 年上半年，直接投资[①] 顺差 139 亿美元，2016 年同期为逆差 494 亿美元（见图 1-6）。其中，直接投资资产净增加 411 亿美元，同比少增 67%；直接投资负债净增加 550 亿美元，同比少增 26%。

证券投资逆差收窄。2017 年上半年，证券投资逆差 195 亿美元，同比下降 41%（见图 1-6）。其中，我国对外证券投资净流出（资产净增加）401 亿美元，增长 6%；境外对我国证券投资净流入（负债净增加）206 亿美元，增长 3.5 倍。

其他投资转为顺差。2017 年上半年，贷款、贸易信贷以及资金存放等其他投资为顺差 732 亿美元，2016 年同期为逆差 938 亿美元（见图 1-6）。其中，我国对外的其他投资净流出（资产净增加）536 亿美元，下降 29%；境外对我国的其他投资净流入（负债净增加）1 267 亿美元，上年同期为净流出 179 亿美元。

储备资产有所增加。2017 年上半年，我国交易形成的储备资产（剔除汇率、价格等非交易价值变动影响）增加 290 亿美元。其中，交易形成的外汇储备资产增加

① 本口径与商务部公布的数据主要差异在于，国际收支统计中还包括了外商投资企业的未分配利润、已分配未汇出利润、盈余公积、股东贷款、金融机构吸收外资、非居民购买不动产等内容。

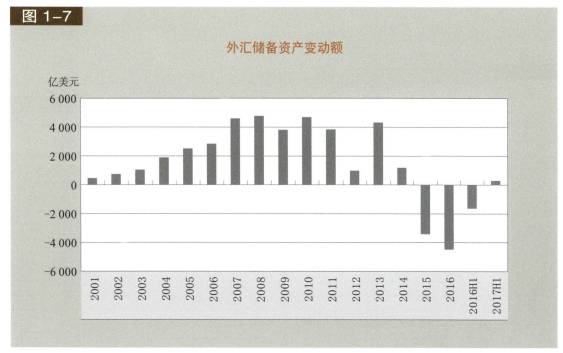

图 1-7

外汇储备资产变动额

数据来源：国家外汇管理局。

294 亿美元（见图 1-7）。截至 2017 年 6 月末，我国外汇储备余额 30 568 亿美元，较上年末余额上升 463 亿美元。

表 1-2 2017 年上半年中国国际收支平衡表   单位：亿美元

项　　目	行次	2017 年上半年
1. 经常账户	1	693
贷方	2	12 680
借方	3	−11 987
1.A 货物和服务	4	793
贷方	5	11 283
借方	6	−10 490
1.A.a 货物	7	2 144
贷方	8	10 269
借方	9	−8 126
1.A.b 服务	10	−1 351
贷方	11	1 014
借方	12	−2 364
1.A.b.1 加工服务	13	87
贷方	14	88
借方	15	−1
1.A.b.2 维护和维修服务	16	18
贷方	17	28
借方	18	−10
1.A.b.3 运输	19	−262
贷方	20	173
借方	21	−435

项　目	行次	2017 年上半年
1．A．b．4 旅行	22	−1 159
贷方	23	188
借方	24	−1 347
1．A．b．5 建设	25	10
贷方	26	53
借方	27	−42
1．A．b．6 保险和养老金服务	28	−33
贷方	29	18
借方	30	−51
1．A．b．7 金融服务	31	8
贷方	32	14
借方	33	−7
1．A．b．8 知识产权使用费	34	−121
贷方	35	22
借方	36	−143
1．A．b．9 电信、计算机和信息服务	37	45
贷方	38	136
借方	39	−91
1．A．b．10 其他商业服务	40	76
贷方	41	282
借方	42	−206
1．A．b．11 个人、文化和娱乐服务	43	−9
贷方	44	4
借方	45	−12
1．A．b．12 别处未提及的政府服务	46	−11
贷方	47	8
借方	48	−19
1．B 初次收入	49	−34
贷方	50	1 250
借方	51	−1 284
1．B．1 雇员报酬	52	85
贷方	53	117
借方	54	−32
1．B．2 投资收益	55	−122
贷方	56	1 130
借方	57	−1 252
1．B．3 其他初次收入	58	2
贷方	59	3
借方	60	−1
1．C 二次收入	61	−67
贷方	62	147
借方	63	−213
2．资本和金融账户	64	389
2.1 资本账户	65	−1
贷方	66	1
借方	67	−2
2.2 金融账户	68	390
资产	69	−1 632
负债	70	2 021
2.2.1 非储备性质的金融账户	71	679
资产	72	−1 342
负债	73	2 021
2.2.1.1 直接投资	74	139
2.2.1.1.1 直接投资资产	75	−411
2.2.1.1.1.1 股权	76	−419
2.2.1.1.1.2 关联企业债务	77	8

续表

项　目	行次	2017 年上半年
2.2.1.1.2 直接投资负债	78	550
2.2.1.1.2.1 股权	79	520
2.2.1.1.2.2 关联企业债务	80	30
2.2.1.2 证券投资	81	−195
2.2.1.2.1 资产	82	−401
2.2.1.2.1.1 股权	83	−142
2.2.1.2.1.2 债券	84	−259
2.2.1.2.2 负债	85	206
2.2.1.2.2.1 股权	86	116
2.2.1.2.2.2 债券	87	90
2.2.1.3 金融衍生工具	88	3
2.2.1.3.1 资产	89	5
2.2.1.3.2 负债	90	−2
2.2.1.4 其他投资	91	732
2.2.1.4.1 资产	92	−536
2.2.1.4.1.1 其他股权	93	−1
2.2.1.4.1.2 货币和存款	94	−83
2.2.1.4.1.3 贷款	95	−665
2.2.1.4.1.4 保险和养老金	96	−3
2.2.1.4.1.5 贸易信贷	97	296
2.2.1.4.1.6 其他	98	−80
2.2.1.4.2 负债	99	1 267
2.2.1.4.2.1 其他股权	100	0
2.2.1.4.2.2 货币和存款	101	995
2.2.1.4.2.3 贷款	102	547
2.2.1.4.2.4 保险和养老金	103	2
2.2.1.4.2.5 贸易信贷	104	−339
2.2.1.4.2.6 其他	105	62
2.2.1.4.2.7 特别提款权	106	0
2.2.2 储备资产	107	−290
2.2.2.1 货币黄金	108	0
2.2.2.2 特别提款权	109	0
2.2.2.3 在国际货币基金组织的储备头寸	110	4
2.2.2.4 外汇储备	111	−294
2.2.2.5 其他储备资产	112	0
3. 净误差与遗漏	113	−1 081

注：1. 本表根据《国际收支和国际投资头寸手册》（第六版）编制。

2. "贷方"按正值列示，"借方"按负值列示，差额等于"贷方"加上"借方"。本表除标注"贷方"和"借方"的项目外，其他项目均指差额。

3. 本表计数采用四舍五入原则。

数据来源：国家外汇管理局。

（三）国际收支运行评价

经常账户顺差规模仍然处于合理区间。2017 年上半年，我国经常账户顺差与 GDP 之比为 1.2%，依然处于合理区间。其中，第一季度经常账户顺差与 GDP 之比为 0.7%，第二季度为 1.7%。分项目看，2017 年上半年，货物贸易差额与 GDP 之比为 3.9%，服务贸易差额与 GDP 之比为 –2.4%，初次收入和二次收入合计差额与 GDP 之比为 –0.2%（见图 1–8）。

图 1-8

经常账户差额与 GDP 之比及其结构

数据来源：国家外汇管理局、国家统计局。

图 1-9

国际收支差额与外汇储备资产变动

数据来源：国家外汇管理局。

跨境资本流动形势回稳向好。2017 年上半年，非储备性质的金融账户顺差 679 亿美元，上年同期为逆差 1 787 亿美元。自 2014 年第二季度以来，非储备性质的金融账户连续 11 个季度均为逆差，2017 年第一季度重现顺差 368 亿美元，第二季度顺差 311 亿美元。受此影响，2017 年上半年交易形成的外汇储备资产稳中有升，我国国际收支总体呈现自主平衡格局（见图 1–9）。

境内主体对外投资更加理性有序。2017 年上半年，境内主体对外直接投资、证券投资和其他投资等资产合计净增加 1 342 亿美元，同比少增 45%（见图 1–10）。其中，第一季度对外投资资产净增加 547 亿美元，第二季度净增加 795 亿美元。首先，对外直接投资逐步向理性回归。上半年，直接投资资产净增加 411 亿美元，同比少增 67%，但依然保持一定规模，说明当前一些非理性的对外投资得到有效遏制，正常的企业"走出去"继续获得有力支持。其次，对外证券投资平稳增长。境外股权、债券等相关资产合计净增加 401 亿美元，同比多增 6%。此外，对外存款、贷款等其他投资资产净增加 536 亿美元，同比少增 29%。

境外主体来华各类投资较快回升。2017 年上半年，外国来华直接投资、证券投资和其他投资等外来投资净流入（即对外负债净增加）2 021 亿美元，同比上升 2.2 倍（见图 1–10）。其中，第一季度净流入 915 亿美元，第二季度净流入 1 106 亿美

图 1–10

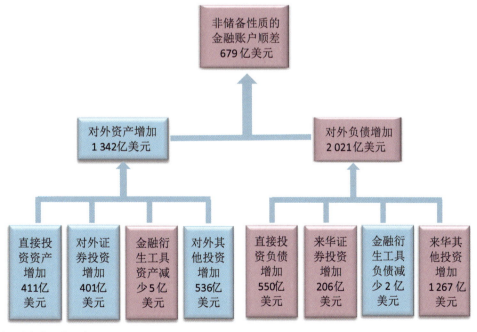

2017 年上半年中国跨境资本流动的结构分析

数据来源：国家外汇管理局。

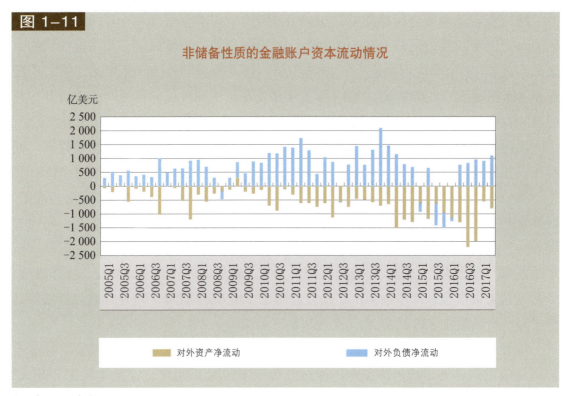

图 1-11

非储备性质的金融账户资本流动情况

亿美元

数据来源：国家外汇管理局。

元。一方面，境外投资者持续增加对我国投资。直接投资项下境外资本保持一定规模净流入，上半年为 550 亿美元；同时，随着境内资本市场对外开放深入推进，来华证券投资规模不断提高，上半年净流入 206 亿美元，同比增加 3.5 倍，其中，第一季度净流入 68 亿美元，第二季度净流入 138 亿美元。此外，境外投资者持有境内人民币等存款资产意愿继续上升，货币和存款项下资金净流入 995 亿美元，同比增长 3.5 倍。另一方面，境内主体融资意愿强烈，跨境融资需求持续回升。自 2016 年第二季度以来，境内主体吸收的境外贷款持续 5 个季度呈现资金净流入，且规模逐渐提升，上半年累计净流入 547 亿美元，2016 年同期为净流出 318 亿美元（见图 1-11）。

国内外因素共同推动我国国际收支趋向基本平衡。从国内看，第一，经济稳中向好的发展态势更加明显，经济增速在世界范围内仍保持较高水平，很多经济指标持续向好，有助于提振市场信心；第二，人民币对美元汇率双向波动明显增强，随着中间价形成机制进一步完善，逆周期调节效果初步显现，市场主体预期进一步趋稳，相关购付汇行为趋向基本稳定；第三，国内市场更加开放，外资进入中国市场积极性和信心进一步增强。从国外看，国际金融市场相对稳定，美联储加息等市场冲击逐步减弱，市场主体对相关影响的应对和适应能力有所增强。总体来看，当前我国国际收支平衡的基础更加稳固。

经济新常态下我国国际收支运行保持稳健

近年来，国内外经济金融环境发生较大变化。全球经济增长出现分化，发达经济体经济缓慢复苏，新兴经济体经济增速回落；主要发达经济体货币政策转向，国际金融市场受到较大影响。同时，国内经济发展进入新常态。党的十八大以来，面对错综复杂的国内外环境，以习近平同志为核心的党中央审时度势，开拓创新，砥砺奋进，保持国内经济始终运行在合理区间，推动供给侧结构性改革，开创对外开放新局面，积极防范跨境资本流动风险，为我国国际收支抵御外部冲击、趋向基本平衡奠定了坚实的基础。

经常账户顺差始终处于合理区间且更趋平衡，体现了国内经济结构的优化调整。近十年，我国经常账户收支状况逐渐走向平衡，经常账户顺差与GDP之比由2007年的近10%降至2010年以来的4%以下，长期处于一个比较合理的水平。2013—2016年，经常账户顺差与GDP之比年均2.1%，2017年上半年为1.2%，比2012年之前更趋平衡。党的十八大提出，要使经济发展更多依靠内需特别是消费需求拉动。2013—2016年，最终消费支出对我国经济增长的年均贡献率为55%，总体呈现稳中有升的发展态势，2017年上半年贡献率为63%。居民消费的增强必然带动居民储蓄水平的下降，有助于收敛我国储蓄高于投资的缺口（对应经常账户差额，见图C2-1）。从具体项目看，货物贸易保持一定规模顺差，近期在内需拉动下进口增长相对较快、顺差有所下降；服务贸易尤其是旅行项下逆差较快上升，主要体现了居民收入水平不断提升、出境政策更加便利、境外旅游留学等消费需求持续高涨的影响。2016年，我国出境人数达1.35亿人次，是2012年的1.6倍；出国留学人员达54万人，是2012年的1.4倍。

跨境资本流动在双向波动中趋向稳定，有效应对了外部环境的重大变化。2013年，我国非储备性质金融账户顺差3 430亿美元，2014年出现514亿美元小幅逆差，2015年和2016年每年的逆差规模均超过4 000亿美元，2017年上半年重新转为顺差679亿美元。一方面，我国对外直接投资、证券投资和其他投资较快增长，2017年以来境内主体更趋理性，对外直接投资有所回落。

图 C2-1

消费对经济增长贡献率和经常账户差额与 GDP 之比

图例：
■ 最终消费支出对经济增长贡献率（左轴）　—— 经常账户差额／GDP（右轴）

数据来源：国家统计局，国家外汇管理局。

另一方面，外国来华直接投资总体稳定，对外负债在经历一段时期去杠杆后恢复增长。我国跨境资本流动变化具有深刻的国际背景，同时也体现了国内基本面的支撑作用。2008 年国际金融危机爆发以来，主要发达经济体实施极度宽松的货币政策，我国等新兴经济体普遍面临资本流入压力。但 2014 年以来国际环境发生重大转变，美联储退出量化宽松货币政策并启动加息进程，部分新兴经济体国内经济、政治等问题迭出，跨境资本开始从新兴经济体流出。在复杂严峻的国际环境下，党中央国务院始终坚持稳中求进的工作总基调，保持国内经济平稳运行和社会大局稳定，守住不发生区域性、系统性风险的底线，为我国跨境资本流动逐步企稳奠定了坚实的基础。

国际收支风险总体可控，对外金融资产负债结构有所优化。我国基础的国际清偿能力持续较强，国际收支支付风险较低，经常账户持续顺差，外汇储备仍较充裕。外汇储备余额能够支付 20 多个月的进口，远高于"不低于 3~4 个月"的国际警戒标准；相当于本外币短期外债的 3 倍以上，远高于

"不低于1倍"的警戒标准。同时，外债风险总体可控。近5年，外债余额先升后降再平稳恢复，释放了部分偿债压力。截至2017年第二季度末，我国本外币全口径外债余额已连续5个季度增长，但仍低于2014年末的历史较高水平。负债率、债务率、偿债率等衡量外债风险的指标持续处于国际警戒标准之内。此外，近年来，民间部门持有的对外资产比例由2012年末的35%上升到2017年第二季度末的53%，使其对外资产和负债的匹配度趋向改善，有利于防范相关风险。2017年第二季度末，民间部门对外净负债1.40万亿美元，比2012年末下降1 225亿美元。

未来，我国经济社会健康发展的基础更加稳固，国内市场开放程度进一步加深，市场主体涉外交易更趋平稳，将推动我国国际收支保持基本平衡。

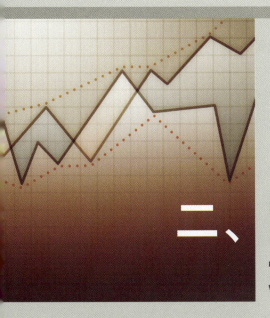

二、国际收支主要
项目分析

（一）货物贸易

货物贸易进出口总额回升，外贸依存度略有增加。据海关统计，2017 年上半年，我国进出口总额 1.9 万亿美元，同比增长 13%，外贸依存度（即进出口总额／GDP）为 34%，同比上升 2 个百分点（见图 2-1），反映了随着全球经济形势回暖，我国外贸增长进一步拉动全球贸易复苏。进出口顺差 1 833 亿美元，下降 24%，主要是 2017 年以来国内经济总体稳中向好，主要大宗商品进口价格同比有所反弹。

受国内外需求回暖等影响，进出口数量和价格指数均出现上升。2017 年上半年，外部需求回暖带动出口量价齐升。根据海关统计，出口价格指数月均上涨 5%，出口数量指数月均上涨 9%。同时，受国内经济增速稳中有升提振作用和大宗商品价格整体上涨影响，上半年进口数量指数月均增长 12%，进口价格指数月均增长 13%。

货物贸易跨境收支顺差下降，跨境外汇保持较大净流入。2017 年上半年，我国货物贸易跨境收入 9 654 亿美元，同比上升 5%；跨境支出 8 860 亿美元，同比上升 14%；收支顺差 794 亿美元，下降 46%（见图 2-2）。其中，跨境外汇收支顺差 1 128 亿美元，同比下降 12%。

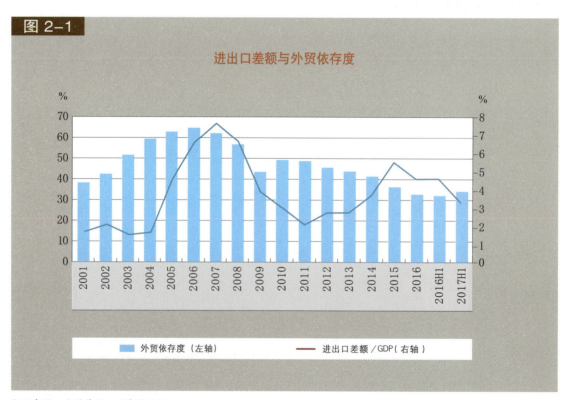

图 2-1

进出口差额与外贸依存度

外贸依存度（左轴）　　　进出口差额／GDP（右轴）

数据来源：海关总署、国家统计局。

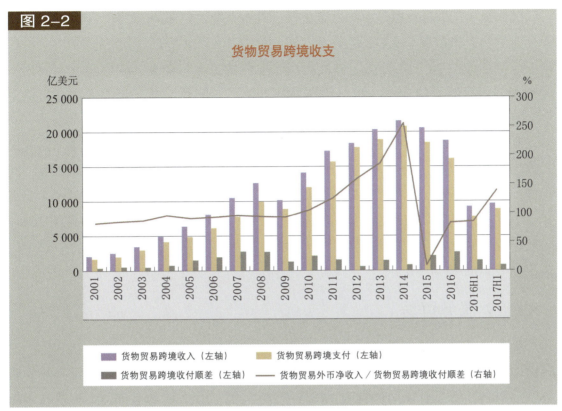

图 2-2

货物贸易跨境收支

注：货物贸易跨境收支为海关统计口径。
数据来源：国家外汇管理局。

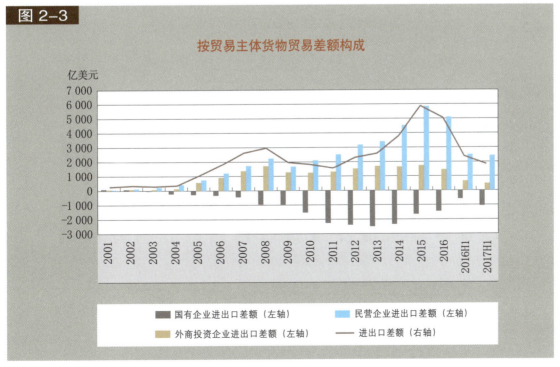

图 2-3

按贸易主体货物贸易差额构成

数据来源：海关总署。

民营企业在进出口顺差中的比重上升，外资企业占比略降。2017 年上半年，民营企业货物进出口顺差 2 428 亿美元，同比下降 3%，相当于总顺差的 131%，占比较上年同期增加 34 个百分点；外商投资企业货物进出口顺差 487 亿美元，同比下降 26%，占总顺差的 26%，与上年同期基本持平。此外，国有企业货物进出口逆差 1 065 亿美元，同比上升 82%（见图 2-3）。

我国出口商品在主要发达经济体的份额相对稳定，对部分"一带一路"沿线国家进出口快速增长。2017 年上半年，美国进口商品中来自中国的比重为 20%，同比增加 0.2 个百分点；欧盟进口商品中来自中国的比重为 19%，同比减少 0.7 个百分点；日本进口商品中来自中国的比重为 24%，同比减少 2 个百分点（见图 2-4）。同期，我国对俄罗斯、巴基斯坦、波兰和哈萨克斯坦等国进出口分别增长 33.1%、14.5%、24.6% 和 46.8%。

（二）服务贸易

服务贸易总规模增长。2017 年上半年，我国服务贸易收支总额 3 378 亿美元，同比增长 9%。同期货物贸易总额为 18 395 亿美元，增长 15%。2017 年上半年，服务贸易与货物贸易总额的比例为 18%（见图 2-5）。2017 年上半年，服务贸易中保

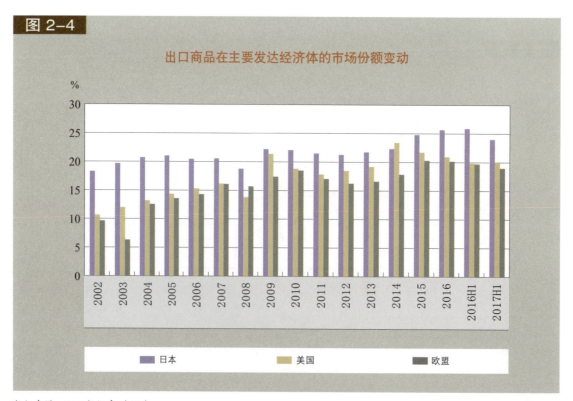

图 2-4

出口商品在主要发达经济体的市场份额变动

数据来源：环亚数据库（CEIC）。

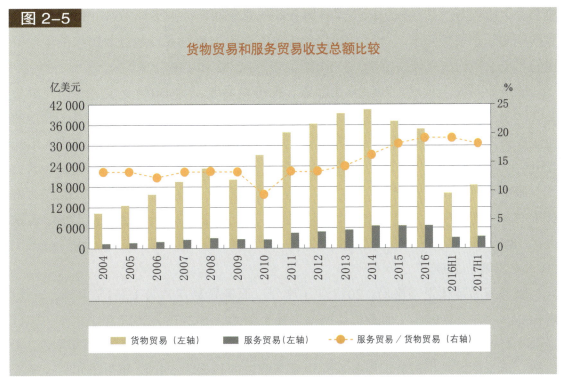

图2-5

货物贸易和服务贸易收支总额比较

数据来源：国家外汇管理局。

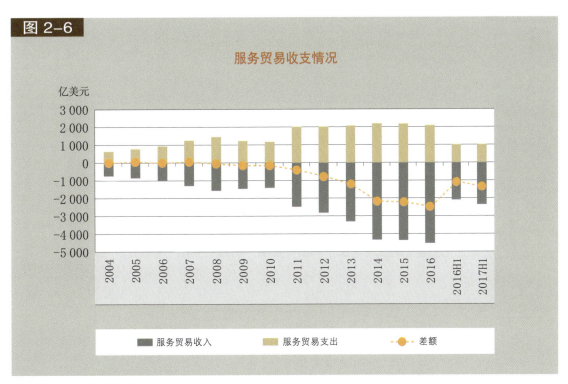

图2-6

服务贸易收支情况

数据来源：国家外汇管理局。

险和养老金服务、金融服务以及建设服务收支总额同比分别下降 16%、15% 和 8%，而同期知识产权使用费、计算机和信息服务等高附加值服务贸易以及传统的运输行业的收支总额均出现较高增速，分别增长 36%、23% 和 15%。

服务贸易收入微增。 2017 年上半年，服务贸易收入为 1 014 亿美元，同比增长 0.4%（见图 2-6）。占服务贸易收入比重较大的项目中，旅行收入下降 12%，其他商业服务下降 1%，运输增长 8%；其他占比较小的项目中，知识产权使用费收入增长 4.5 倍。

服务贸易支出保持增长。 2017 年上半年，服务贸易支出 2 364 亿美元，同比增长 13%。占服务贸易支出比重较大的项目中，旅行占比 57%，支出增长 13%；运输占比 18%，支出增长 18%；其他商业服务占比为 9%，支出下降 5%；知识产权占比 6%，支出增长 22%。

服务贸易延续逆差格局。 2017 年上半年，服务贸易逆差为 1 351 亿美元，同比增长 24%，旅行逆差仍为服务贸易逆差主要来源（见图 2-7）。2017 年上半年，旅行逆差 1 159 亿美元，增长 19%。随着我国经济发展和国民收入提高，我国居民出国旅游、留学的需求仍较大。服务逆差中排名第二的是运输，2017 年上半年，运输逆差 262 亿美元，增长 26%，上半年我国进口增幅较大，货运运输支出随之增长，导致运输逆差上升。

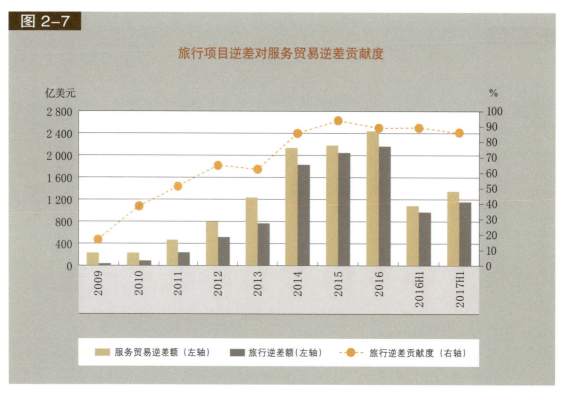

图 2-7

旅行项目逆差对服务贸易逆差贡献度

数据来源：国家外汇管理局。

图 2-8

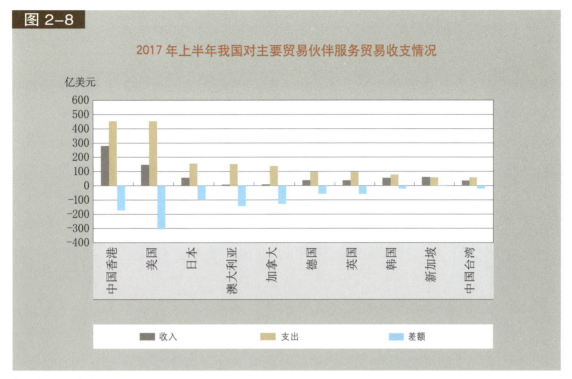

2017 年上半年我国对主要贸易伙伴服务贸易收支情况

亿美元

图例：■ 收入　　■ 支出　　■ 差额

数据来源：国家外汇管理局。

　　逆差国家和地区保持高集中度趋势。 2017 年上半年，我国服务贸易前十大伙伴国（地区）依次为中国香港、美国、日本、澳大利亚、加拿大、德国、英国、韩国、新加坡和中国台湾，贸易规模达 2 464 亿美元，占服务贸易总规模的 73%。其中，除对新加坡为顺差外，我国对其余九个主要贸易伙伴国（地区）的服务贸易均呈逆差，对中国香港、美国、澳大利亚和加拿大的逆差均超百亿美元规模（见图 2-8）。2017 年上半年，我国对美国服务贸易逆差规模最大，然后依次是中国香港、澳大利亚、加拿大和日本。

专栏 3

创新外汇管理方式，支持跨境电子商务发展

　　在经济一体化、贸易全球化的背景下，跨境电子商务正在引起国际贸易方式的巨大变革。对企业来说，极大地拓宽了进入国际市场的路径，促进了多边资源的优化配置与企业间互利共赢；对于消费者来说，跨境电子商务使人们更容易获取其他国家的商品及服务，满足个人的消费需求。

近年来，我国跨境电子商务业务快速发展。据中国电子商务研究中心数据显示，2016 年，中国跨境电子商务交易规模达 6 万亿元，同比增长 16.7%。我国跨境电子商务平台企业超过 5 000 家，通过跨境电子商务平台开展跨境电子商务业务的企业超过 20 万家。与传统贸易相比，我国跨境电子商务交易呈现小额、分散等特点，尤其在便利性方面更加突出：一是买卖双方通过网络等线上渠道直接撮合，减少中间环节，更加便捷高效；二是随着参与主体准入门槛的降低，交易主体更加多元化，包括小微企业、个人商户等；三是结算渠道不断创新，可通过线上银行卡、第三方支付机构、线下银行结算等；四是跨境电子商务模式呈现多样化，具体来看：

进口业务项下主要模式包括：一般贸易模式，境内电子商务平台线上取得订单后，以传统外贸形式报关进口；个人海淘等邮包进口模式，消费者通过境外电子商务网站购买商品，境外供应商通过邮包等方式将商品邮寄至境内消费者；保税备货模式，跨境电子商务平台提前备货至保税区，在消费者下单后，保税区仓储企业直接向海关申报后配送给消费者。

出口业务项下主要模式包括：综合试验区模式，在跨境电子商务综合试验区内，海关简化出口报关手续，出口采取"清单核放、汇总申报"的方式，即将商品先邮寄给境外消费者，再定期将邮寄出口商品汇总统计；直接邮包出口模式，部分电商卖家直接以邮包方式发货；出口"海外仓"模式，国内电商在境外成立关联公司，并以"一般贸易"形式集中出口发货至海外仓，海外仓再负责国外消费者订单配送。

外汇管理进一步便利跨境电子商务外汇资金结算。目前，全国跨境电子商务综合试验区已落地杭州、天津等 13 个城市。在政策层面上，对跨境电子商务在关、检、税、汇等方面给予便利。在外汇方面：一是推动支付机构跨境电子商务外汇支付业务试点。2015 年，支付机构跨境电子商务外汇支付业务试点范围扩大至全国，放开地区限制、下放审核权限、提高单笔限额、扩大支付范围。二是允许从事跨境电子商务业务的个体工商户开立个人外汇结算账户，打造阳光化的收结汇通道。在风险可控的基础上，外汇局将继续提升跨境电子商务外汇资金结算的便利化水平，大力支持跨境电子商务等外贸新业态健康蓬勃发展。

（三）直接投资

直接投资由净流出转为净流入[①]。2017 年上半年，我国国际收支口径的直接投资净流入 139 亿美元（见图 2-9），上年同期为净流出 494 亿美元。直接投资项下由持续净流出转变为净流入，一方面是由于我国企业对外直接投资更趋理性、境外资产配置进程趋缓；另一方面，外国来华直接投资继续呈现较大净流入。

直接投资资产[②]**增幅趋缓**。2017 年上半年，我国直接投资资产（主要是我国对外直接投资）净增加 411 亿美元，同比少增 67%（见图 2-10）。

从投资形式看，一是股权投资类资产净增加 419 亿美元，同比少增 48%。直接投资中的股权投资属于长期投资，此类交易增幅明显趋缓表明，随着国内经济持续向好和国际环境不稳定、不确定因素仍然很多，境内企业在经过多年的对外直接投资高速增长后，更趋理性看待对外长期投资。二是对境外关联公司贷款等资产净减少 8 亿美元，上年同期为净增加 431 亿美元，反映此类投资灵活多变，易受短期市场因素影响。

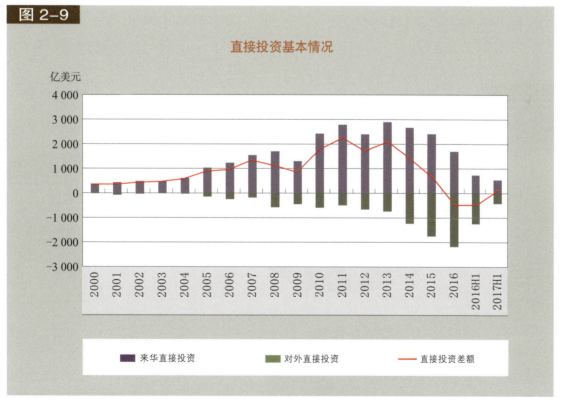

图 2-9

直接投资基本情况

亿美元

■ 来华直接投资　　■ 对外直接投资　　— 直接投资差额

数据来源：国家外汇管理局。

---

① 直接投资净流动指直接投资资产净增加额（资金净流出）与直接投资负债净增加额（资金净流入）之差。当直接投资资产净增加额大于直接投资负债净增加额时，直接投资项目为净流出。反之，则直接投资项目为净流入。

② 直接投资资产以我国对外直接投资为主，但也包括少量境内外商投资企业对境外母公司的反向投资等。

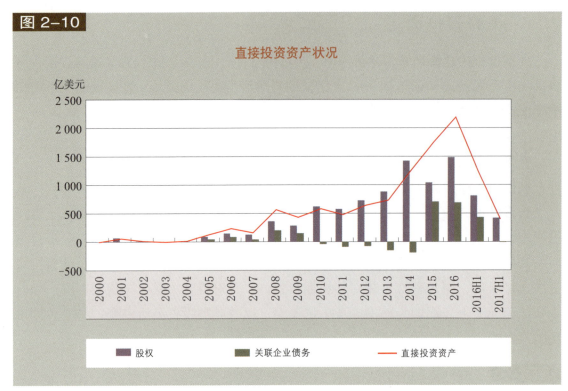

图 2-10

直接投资资产状况

数据来源：国家外汇管理局。

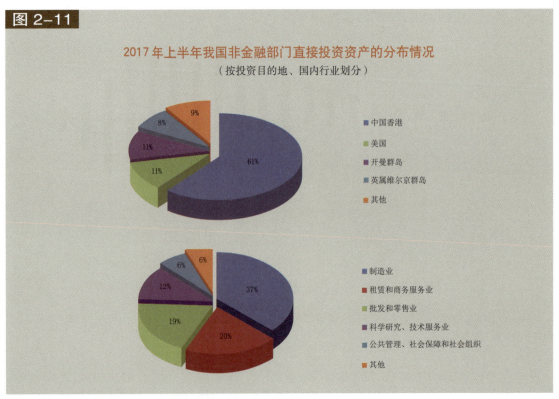

图 2-11

2017 年上半年我国非金融部门直接投资资产的分布情况
（按投资目的地、国内行业划分）

数据来源：国家外汇管理局。

分部门看，一是非金融部门的直接投资资产净增加 318 亿美元，同比少增 71%。境内企业新增对外直接投资目的地仍主要集中于中国香港，占比逾六成，其次是美国和开曼群岛，两者合计占比 22%，"走出去"目的地相对集中在资金进出管理相对宽松的国家/地区，这与全球股权投资模式与渠道一致。在国内"走出去"的行业中，制造业由上年同期的第二位升至首位，占比为 37%，较上年增长 14 个百分点；其次是租赁和商务服务业，占比为 20%，较上年下降 3 个百分点（见图 2–11）。二是金融部门的直接投资资产净增加 93 亿美元，同比少增 41%，主要是银行部门和其他金融业的对外直接投资。

直接投资负债① 继续保持较大净流入。2017 年上半年，直接投资负债净增加 550 亿美元，同比少增 26%。

从投资形式看，一是股权投资类负债净增加 520 亿美元，同比少增 32%（见图 2–12）。在我国投资环境不断改善的情况下，来华直接投资中股权投资保持稳定表明外资仍保持长期投资中国的信心。二是接受境外关联公司贷款等负债净增加 30 亿美元，上年同期为净减少 20 亿美元，这主要是企业根据境内外两个市场因素进行财务运作的结果。

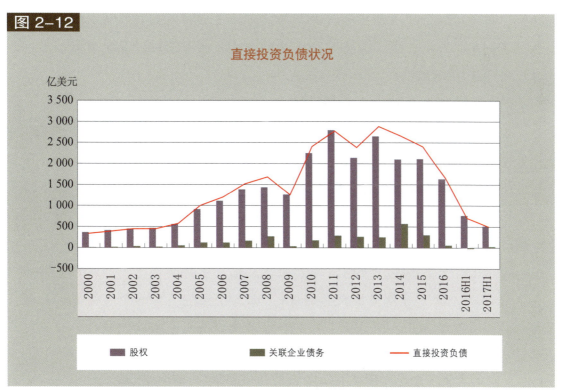

图 2-12
直接投资负债状况

数据来源：国家外汇管理局。

---

① 直接投资负债以吸收来华直接投资为主，但也包括少量境外子公司对境内母公司的反向投资等。

分部门看，一是非金融部门的直接投资负债净增加 497 亿美元，同比少增 29%，占新增直接投资负债的九成。随着我国经济结构转型的不断推进，境外股东不断调整其投向。2017 年上半年，租赁和商务服务业重新成为非金融部门吸收直接投资最多的行业，占比 28%，较上年同期上升 19 个百分点；批发和零售业排第二位，占 26%，较上年同期上升 14 个百分点；房地产业吸收的直接投资由上年的净增加转为净减少。同时，对我国直接投资最多的国家 / 地区仍是中国香港，其次是荷兰、中国台湾和韩国，前四名的排名与上年同期一致。二是金融部门的直接投资负债净增加 53 亿美元，同比多增 13%，绝大多数投向银行业，且主要为收益再投资，说明境内银行业经营状况较好，境外机构继续增加投资。

专栏 4

2017 年上半年对外直接投资总量放缓结构优化

在经历 2015 年和 2016 年的扩张之后，受基数较高、国内外经济形势变化等影响，2017 年上半年，我国对外直接投资总量有所放缓，但对外投资的结构、质量得到进一步优化和提升。当前市场主体对外直接投资趋向稳定有序，下一步，外汇管理部门将继续保持对外直接投资管理政策的稳定性，并积极研究适应新情况。

一、2017 年上半年对外直接投资结构有所优化

从增速看，据商务部统计（下同），2017 年上半年，我国非金融企业对境外房地产业、文化、体育和娱乐业的直接投资合计 15 亿美元，同比下降 82%；若剔除上述行业数据，非金融类对外直接投资 467 亿美元，同比下降 37%。正常的对外直接投资能够一如既往地按现行有关规定办理对外投资登记和购付汇手续。

从占比看，上半年，流向房地产业、文化、体育和娱乐业的对外直接投资占同期非金融类对外直接投资的 3%，比上年同期下降 6 个百分点，而流向租赁和商业服务业、制造业、批发和零售业以及信息传输、软件和信息技术服务业的资金占比整体较上年同期有所提升，分别为 28%、18%、13% 和 11%，对外投资的结构和质量总体得到进一步提升。

从国家地区分布看，2017 年上半年，我国企业对"一带一路"沿线的 47 个国

家新增投资 66 亿美元，占同期对外投资总额的 14%，比去年同期增加 6 个百分点。

二、对外直接投资结构优化与国内外经济环境变化和政策规范等密切相关

一是国内宏观经济稳中向好、人民币汇率稳中趋升，弱化了市场主体对外投资和配置海外资产的动力。一方面，2017 年以来，我国国内生产总值、居民消费价格、城镇新增就业、国际收支等主要经济指标均好于预期，企业和个人对国内经济发展信心增强；另一方面，人民币对美元汇率双向波动明显，上半年中间价累计升值 2.4%，同时，人民币对美元汇率中间价形成机制进一步完善，逆周期调节效果初步显现。在此情况下，境内主体对外投资更趋理性，更多资金选择留在国内。

二是规范对外直接投资的措施效果显现。为促进我国对外直接投资健康发展，在推动对外投资便利化的同时，国家发展改革委、商务部、人民银行、外汇局等对一些具有非理性的投资加强真实性、合规性审核，对外投资结构进一步优化，涉及房地产、酒店、影城、娱乐业、体育俱乐部等领域的对外投资大幅下降。2017 年以来外汇管理部门根据形势变化，不断调整完善相关措施，目前对外投资外汇管理政策已基本回归常态，企业用汇需求平稳可控。

此外，欧美国家通过外资安全审查等方式对部分并购项目干预增多，一定程度上也影响了境内主体开展对外投资。

下一步，外汇管理部门将会同对外投资管理有关部门继续支持有条件、有能力的境内企业开展真实合规的对外直接投资，积极支持推进"一带一路"建设和国际产能合作。同时，坚持便利化和防风险并重，继续引导境内企业理性投资，指导金融机构加强跨境并购贷款和内保外贷业务的合规管理和风险管理，严厉打击虚假担保和恶意担保等违规行为，在促进对外投资健康有序发展的同时，有效维护涉外金融安全。

（四）证券投资

证券投资总体呈现净流出，但规模回落。2017 年上半年，我国证券投资项下净流出 195 亿美元，同比下降 41%（见图 2-13），主要是境外对我证券投资大幅流入所致。从交易工具看，2017 年上半年，股权和债券投资分别净流出 25 亿美元和 170 亿美元，同比分别回落 80% 和 16%。

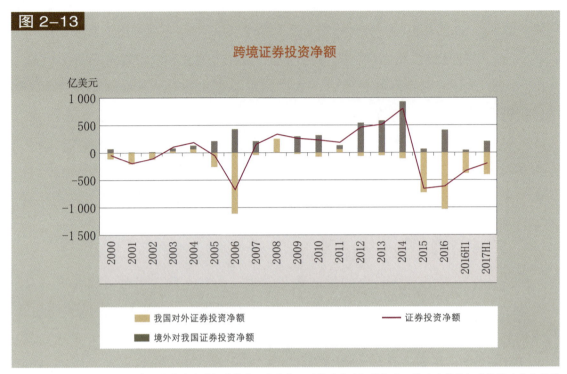

图 2-13

跨境证券投资净额

亿美元

图例：
- 我国对外证券投资净额
- 境外对我国证券投资净额
- 证券投资净额

注：我国对外证券投资正值表示减持对外股权或债券，负值表示增持对外股权或债券；境外对我国证券投资正值表示增加对国内股权或债权投资，负值表示减少对国内股权或债券投资。

数据来源：国家外汇管理局。

对境外证券投资小幅增加。 2017 年上半年，我国对外证券投资增加（净流出）401 亿美元，同比多增 6%。其中，股权投资增加 142 亿美元，债券投资增加 259 亿美元。

从对外证券投资的渠道看，一是国内居民通过"港股通"和"基金互认"等渠道购买境外证券类资产 180 亿美元；二是境内银行等金融机构投资境外股票和债券 155 亿美元；三是合格境内机构投资者（QDII 及 RQDII）投资非居民发行的股票和债券合计 41 亿美元；四是我国居民购买非居民境内发行债券 25 亿美元。

境外对我国证券投资净流入上升。 2017 年上半年，境外对我国证券投资净流入 206 亿美元，同比增长 3.5 倍，人民币资产在全球资产配置中的吸引力显著增强。其中，境外对我国股权投资净流入 116 亿美元，同比增长 87%；债券投资净流入 90 亿美元，上年同期为净流出 16 亿美元。2017 年，我国进一步开放银行间债券市场，以及中国 A 股纳入明晟新兴市场指数（MSCI），在资本流入和市场信心等方面发挥了积极作用。

从境外对我国证券投资的主要渠道看，一是"沪股通"和"深股通"渠道流入资金 147 亿美元；二是非居民购买我国机构境外发行的股票、债券 103 亿美元；三是境外机构投资境内债券市场 80 亿美元。此外，合格境外机构投资者（QFII）和人民币合格境外机构投资者（RQFII）对境内证券投资减少 115 亿美元；银行承兑远期信用证（附汇票）余额下降形成资金净流出 9 亿美元。

（五）其他投资

其他投资总体呈现净流入。2017 年上半年，我国其他投资项下净负债增加（净流入）732 亿美元，是金融账户净负债增加 390 亿美元的 1.88 倍，而上年同期为净资产增加 938 亿美元（见图 2-14）。其中，货币和存款净负债增加 913 亿美元；贷款净资产增加 118 亿美元；贸易信贷净负债减少 43 亿美元。

其他投资项下资产增幅回落。2017 年上半年，我国其他投资项下对外资产增长 536 亿美元，较上年少增 29%。境内主体参与国际经济活动较为活跃，但增幅下降。我国境外投资趋于稳定，这与人民币汇率双向波动加强和市场主体回归理性有关。2017 年上半年，除直接投资和证券投资以外的对外资本输出主要体现为对境外贷款增加以及货币存款增加，金额分别为 665 亿美元和 83 亿美元，而贸易信贷表现为资

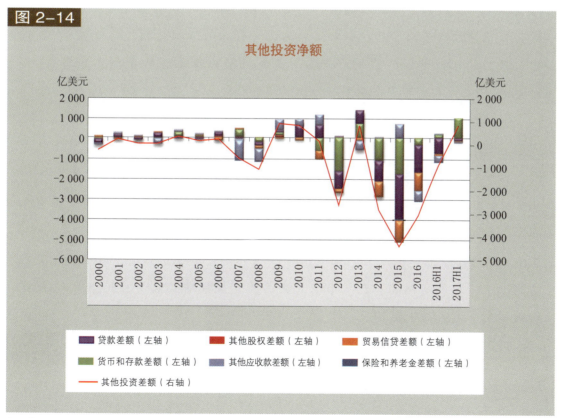

图 2-14

其他投资净额

图例：
- 贷款差额（左轴）
- 其他股权差额（左轴）
- 贸易信贷差额（左轴）
- 货币和存款差额（左轴）
- 其他应收款差额（左轴）
- 保险和养老金差额（左轴）
- 其他投资差额（右轴）

数据来源：国家外汇管理局。

产余额下降（即贸易应收和预付余额下降），为296亿美元。

其他投资项下负债由减转增。2017年上半年，我国其他投资项下对外负债增加1 267亿美元，上年同期为对外负债减少179亿美元。主要变化项目有：一是我国获得境外贷款开始止跌回升，上半年增加547亿美元，上年同期为减少318亿美元。我国企业利用外部贷款积极性提升，表明我国经济形势好转，市场信心增强。二是货币和存款增加995亿美元，同比多增3.5倍，其中，非居民人民币存款2017年上半年增长486亿美元，而2016年上半年下降81亿美元。非居民人民币存款的大幅增长，反映了境外投资者持有人民币资产的意愿回升。三是贸易信贷负债减少339亿美元，较上年多减10%。

专栏5

中国与"一带一路"国家的经济交往日益加深

2013年，我国提出了共建丝绸之路经济带和共建21世纪海上丝绸之路的倡议。目前，已经有60多个国家和国际组织积极响应"一带一路"的倡议。经过四年的发展和合作，我国与"一带一路"沿线国家的经济交往日益加深，贸易和投资活动较为活跃。据外汇局的银行代客涉外收付款统计[①]显示，2016年，我国非银行部门与"一带一路"沿线国家的各类交易资金总量超1.1万亿美元，2017年上半年交易资金总量近6 000亿美元。

中国与"一带一路"沿线国家总体经贸往来更加频繁。2013—2016年，我国非银行部门与"一带一路"沿线国家的各类交易资金总量近4.8万亿美元，占同期我国跨境收支总量的19%。其中，收入2.4万亿美元，占总收入的20%；支出2.3万亿美元，占总支出的18%。其中，交易量最大的两个国家分别是新加坡和韩国，2013—2016年，与上述两国的年均收支总量分别在5 000亿美元和2 000亿美元以上。从增速看，与中国交易收支年均量超100亿美元的国家中，我国与越南、巴基斯坦的交易收支规模增长最快，2016年较2013年均增长了1.5倍左右。

货物贸易往来更加密切。2016年，中国货物贸易资金收支总额为39 054

[①] 跨境收支统计不同于国际收支平衡表和国际投资头寸表的统计口径，其主要是指境内非银行部门居民机构和个人通过境内银行与非居民机构和个人之间发生的收付款。

亿美元，其中，与"一带一路"沿线国家的货物贸易收支为 8 627 亿美元，占比 22%，较 2013 年占比上升 2 个百分点。受外需不足、大宗商品价格下降以及美元加息等多重因素影响，2016 年我国整体货物贸易收支规模较 2013 年下滑 13%，受此影响，与"一带一路"国家的货物贸易也相应下降，但降幅为 6%，远低于整体水平。

以建设和旅行为代表的服务贸易往来进一步深入。 2016 年，中国与"一带一路"沿线国家的服务贸易收支总量为 825 亿美元，较 2013 年增长 25%。服务贸易中，收支规模排名第一的是旅行（包括留学和旅游），金额为 249 亿美元，较 2013 年增长 44%。随着对"一带一路"的宣传，中国人对沿线国家的了解加深，旅游支出随之快速增长。从增长幅度看，增速最快的是建设（多数与基础设施建设相关），2016 年建设收支总量 92 亿美元，较 2013 年增长 98%。在"一带一路"倡议下，中国与沿线国家各自发挥比较优势，取长补短。中国加大国际产能合作，提供了更多的基础设施建设服务。

投融资更加活跃。 2016 年，我国与"一带一路"国家间相互投资的跨境资金总量达 1 784 亿美元，较 2013 年大幅增长 95%，较整体增速高出 4 个百分点。我国与"一带一路"国家投融资往来的加强主要是由于国家开发银行、亚洲基础设施建设银行等金融机构加大对相关国家的融资力度，通过买方信贷和优惠贷款等方式，向南亚等国家提供的大型建设工程[①]和贷款增多。

分区域看，我国与东南亚国家的投资往来较密切，资金规模增长也较快。 2016 年我国与东盟十国的投融资往来共计 1 274 亿美元，较 2013 年大幅增长 1.4 倍；与西亚十八国的投资往来 108 亿美元，增长 43%；与中亚五国的投资往来 40 亿美元，增长 43%；与南亚八国的投资往来 36 亿美元，增长 18%。从单个国家看，在与中国投资往来规模 10 亿美元以上的国家中，我国对哈萨克斯坦、新加坡和巴基斯坦的投资往来增长最快，分别增长 2.2 倍、1.5 倍和1.5 倍。

东部仍是对接"一带一路"的主阵地，西部凭借地理位置优势增长较快。 从地区分布看，经济发达地区仍是对接"一带一路"国家的主阵地。2016 年，北京、上海、广东、江苏、浙江五省市与"一带一路"国家跨境

---

① 根据国际收支统计原则，长期的大型境外工程建设属于直接投资范畴。

收支总量 7 616 亿美元，占全部跨境收支的逾六成。对接"一带一路"的西部九省凭借地理优势，与"一带一路"国家的交易往来增长较快，2016 年西部九省收支总量为 660 亿美元，较之 2013 年，广西、云南、甘肃、青海以及宁夏的增速均在两位数，远高于 4% 的全国平均水平。

中国与"一带一路"国家的跨境资金收支无论是总规模还是增长幅度均有不同程度的提升，"一带一路"倡议带来的发展潜能将是巨大的。随着中国与沿线国家在贸易、投资、技术及其他领域的合作加深，"一带一路"将有可能成为世界上跨度最长的经济走廊，这将带来更大的市场空间、更多的就业机会和更广的合作领域。

三、国际投资
头寸状况

图 3-1

对外金融资产、负债及净资产状况

图例：
- 资产－储备资产（左轴）
- 资产－其他投资（左轴）
- 资产－证券投资（左轴）
- 资产－我国对外直接投资（左轴）
- 负债－外国来华直接投资（左轴）
- 负债－证券投资（左轴）
- 负债－其他投资（左轴）
- 净资产（右轴）

数据来源：国家外汇管理局。

对外金融资产和负债 ① 均有所增长。2017 年 6 月末，我国对外金融资产 66 446 亿美元，较上年末（下同）增长 2.8%；对外负债 48 931 亿美元，增长 4.9%；对外净资产为 17 515 亿美元，减少 2.7%（见图 3-1）。

对外资产中储备资产仍居首位，但民间部门持有占比继续上升。2017 年 6 月末，我国对外金融资产中，国际储备资产余额为 31 504 亿美元，较上年末增长 1.7%，其中由交易引起的储备资产余额增加 290 亿美元，由汇率及价格等非交易因素引起的储备资产余额增加 235 亿美元。储备资产占我国对外金融资产总额 47%，继续占据对外资产首位，但比重较上年末减少 1 个百分点；直接投资资产 13 697 亿美元，占资产总额的比重为 21%；证券投资资产 4 143 亿美元，占比 6%；金融衍生工具资产 60 亿美元，占比 0.1%；存贷款等其他投资资产 17 042 亿美元，占比 26%

---

① 对外金融资产和负债包括直接投资、证券投资及存贷款等其他投资。之所以对外直接投资属于金融资产范畴，是因为境内投资者持有的是境外被投资企业的股权，这与证券投资中的股权投资无本质区别，只是直接投资通常持股比例较高，意在影响或控制企业的生产经营活动。反之，外来直接投资则属于对外金融负债范畴，也是境外投资者对外商投资企业的权益。

图 3-2

我国对外资产结构变化

资产－储备资产占比　　　　资产－其他投资占比
资产－直接投资占比　　　　资产－证券投资占比

数据来源：国家外汇管理局。

图 3-3

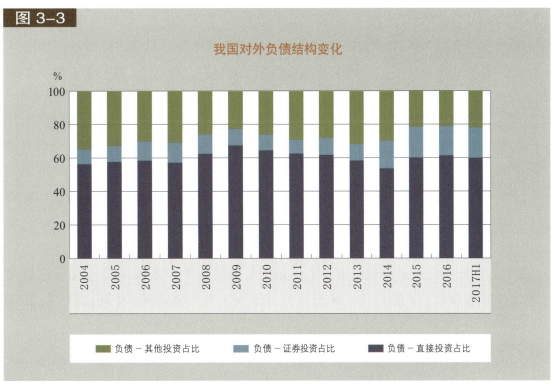

我国对外负债结构变化

负债－其他投资占比　　　负债－证券投资占比　　　负债－直接投资占比

数据来源：国家外汇管理局。

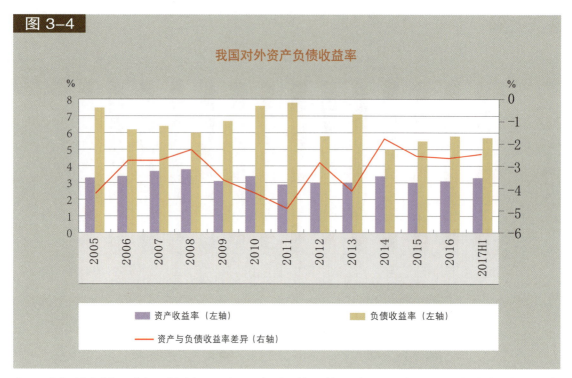

图 3-4

我国对外资产负债收益率

注：1. 资产（或负债）收益率＝[年度投资收益收入（或支出）] ／{[上年末＋本年末对外资产（或负债）存量] ／2}，其中，半年度数据向前累加半年后按照整年计算。
2. 资产负债收益率差异＝资产收益率－负债收益率。
数据来源：国家外汇管理局。

（见图 3-2）。

对外负债仍以外国来华直接投资为主，但来华其他各类投资占比增加。2017 年 6 月末，我国对外负债中，外国来华直接投资 29 245 亿美元[①]，较上年末增长 2%，继续位列对外负债首位，占比 60%，较上年末下降 1 个百分点；证券投资负债 8 583 亿美元，占比 18%，较上年末上升 1 个百分点；金融衍生工具负债 49 亿美元，占比 0.1%；存贷款等其他投资负债 11 054 亿美元，占比 23%，较上年末上升 1 个百分点（见图 3-3）。

对外投资收益差额继续呈现逆差。2017 年上半年，我国国际收支平衡表中投资收益为逆差 122 亿美元，同比下降 41%。其中，我国对外投资收益收入 1 130 亿美元，增长 19%；对外负债收益支出 1 252 亿美元，增长 9%；两者年化收益率差异为 –2.4 个百分点，较上年收窄 0.2 个百分点（见图 3-4）。我国对外金融资产负债结构决定了投资收益差额为负。2017 年 6 月末我国对外金融资产中储备资产占比近

---

① 外国来华直接投资存量包括我国非金融部门和金融部门吸收来华直接投资存量，以及境内外母子公司间贷款和其他债务性往来，并反映了价值重估因素影响。该口径与商务部统计的累计吸收外商直接投资不同，后者是历年外商直接投资股本投资流量累加。

半，因主要为流动性较强的资产，2005 年至 2017 年 6 月我国对外金融资产年平均投资收益率为 3.3%；对外金融负债中主要是外来直接投资，股权投资属于长期、稳定的投资，投资回报一般高于其他形式资产，2005 年至 2017 年 6 月我国对外负债年平均投资收益率为 6.4%。来华直接投资资金持续流入并保持较高的投资收益率，说明我国长期投资环境对于境外投资者仍具有较大的吸引力，来华直接投资在我国经济发展也发挥了积极作用。

专栏 6

国际投资头寸国别比较

国际货币基金组织统计资料显示，2016 年末，我国对外金融资产和负债均较上年末有所回升，对外净资产有所增长，是世界第二大净债权国。

对外资产方面，我国以 6.5 万亿美元位列世界第八，储备资产占比近半；主要发达国家对外资产结构比较均衡，发展中国家则相对单一。发达国家证券投资资产（包含金融衍生品，下同）占比较高，通常在 40% 以上，储备资产占比一般在 5% 以下，其中日本占比相对较高，为 14%（见图 C6-1）。

图 C6-1

2016 年末对外资产构成的国际比较

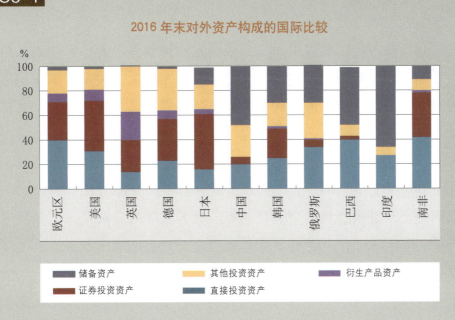

数据来源：国际货币基金组织、国家外汇管理局。

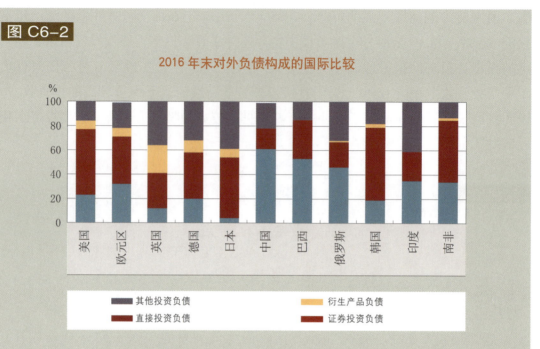

图 C6-2

2016 年末对外负债构成的国际比较

其他投资负债　　　　衍生产品负债
直接投资负债　　　　证券投资负债

数据来源：国际货币基金组织、国家外汇管理局。

而发展中国家储备资产占比一般在 30% 以上，其中我国以 3.1 万亿美元储备资产继续位列世界第一，是排名第二的日本（1.2 万亿美元）储备规模的 2.5 倍；发展中国家证券投资资产占比较低，但韩国和南非占比相对较高，分别为 26% 和 38%。在直接投资资产方面，发达国家和发展中国家占比差异较小。

在对外负债方面，我国以 4.7 万亿美元位列世界第九，来华直接投资占六成；发达国家主要通过证券投资渠道吸收外来资金，发展中国家则以吸收直接投资为主。发达国家开放的金融市场决定了主要通过证券投资渠道吸收外来资金，如美国、日本、英国等发达经济体，证券投资负债（包含金融衍生产品，下同）占总负债的比例均超过 50%（见图 C6-2）。发展中国家主要以吸收直接投资为主，如中国、巴西、俄罗斯占比分别为 61%、53% 和 46%，但韩国和南非例外，直接投资负债较低，证券投资负债较高，证券投资负债占比分别为 63% 和 53%。存贷款等其他投资负债分布较为分散，在主要国家对外负债中的占比 13%~41%。

在对外净资产方面，日本和美国分别为世界上最大净资产国和最大净负债国，我国则以 1.8 万亿美元位列世界第二大净债权国。2016 年末，日本以净资产 3.0 万亿美元，位列净资产第一大国，中国（1.8 万亿美元）和德国（1.8 万亿美元）依次位列第二名和第三名（见表 C6-1）。美国是世界最大的净负债国，2016 年末净负债为 8.1 万亿美元，其次是西班牙和澳大利亚，净负债分别为 1.0 万亿美元和 0.7 万亿美元。虽然英国对外资产和对外负债规模较大，但两者相对接近，净资产规模仅 0.6 万亿美元。

表 C6-1　2016 年末世界主要国家／地区对外资产负债状况　　　　　　　　　　　单位：亿美元

国家（地区）	净资产	资产	负债
日本	29 889	85 424	55 535
中国	18 005	64 666	46 660
德国	17 973	87 092	69 119
中国香港	11 807	45 779	33 973
瑞士	8 393	44 036	35 642
挪威	7 341	15 332	7 991
英国	5 757	136 553	130 796
墨西哥	-4 822	5 824	10 646
爱尔兰	-5 193	51 516	56 709
巴西	-7 166	7 733	14 899
澳大利亚	-7 389	16 111	23 500
西班牙	-10 057	18 688	28 745
美国	-81 096	239 167	320 263

数据来源：国际货币基金组织、国家外汇管理局。

表 3-1　2017 年 6 月末中国国际投资头寸表　　　　　　　　　　　　　　　单位：亿美元

项目	行次	2017 年 6 月末
净头寸①	1	17 515
资产	2	66 446
1 直接投资	3	13 697
1.1 股权	4	11 178
1.2 关联企业债务	5	2 519
1.a 金融部门	6	2 213
1.1.a 股权	7	2 119
1.2.a 关联企业债务	8	94
1.b 非金融部门	9	11 484
1.1.b 股权	10	9 059
1.2.b 关联企业债务	11	2 425
2 证券投资	12	4 143
2.1 股权	13	2 546

① 净头寸是指资产减负债，"＋"表示净资产，"—"表示净负债。本表记数采用四舍五入原则。

项目	行次	2017 年 6 月末
2.2 债券	14	1 597
3 金融衍生工具	15	60
4 其他投资	16	17 042
4.1 其他股权	17	55
4.2 货币和存款	18	3 816
4.3 贷款	19	6 373
4.4 保险和养老金	20	105
4.5 贸易信贷	21	5 849
4.6 其他应收款	22	844
5 储备资产	23	31 504
5.1 货币黄金	24	736
5.2 特别提款权	25	100
5.3 在国际货币基金组织的储备头寸	26	95
5.4 外汇储备	27	30 568
5.5 其他储备	28	5
负债	29	48 931
1 直接投资	30	29 245
1.1 股权	31	27 078
1.2 关联企业债务	32	2 167
1.a 金融部门	33	1 391
1.1.a 股权	34	1 299
1.2.a 关联企业债务	35	92
1.b 非金融部门	36	27 854
1.1.b 股权	37	25 779
1.2.b 关联企业债务	38	2 075
2 证券投资	39	8 583
2.1 股权	40	6 221
2.2 债券	41	2 362
3 金融衍生工具	42	49
4 其他投资	43	11 054
4.1 其他股权	44	0
4.2 货币和存款	45	4 177
4.3 贷款	46	3 910
4.4 保险和养老金	47	95
4.5 贸易信贷	48	2 544
4.6 其他应付款	49	232
4.7 特别提款权	50	97

数据来源：国家外汇管理局。

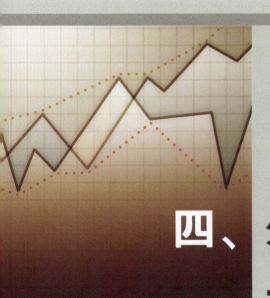

四、外汇市场运行
与人民币汇率

（一）人民币汇率走势

人民币对美元双边汇率升值。2017 年 6 月末，人民币对美元汇率中间价为 6.7744 元 / 美元，较 2016 年末升值 2.4%，境内市场（CNY）和境外市场（CNH）即期交易价累计分别升值 2.4% 和 2.9%（见图 4-1），境内外市场日均价差 189 个基点（见图 4-2），高于 2016 年全年日均价差（134 个基点）。

2017 年 6 月末，人民币对欧元、日元、英镑、澳元、加元汇率中间价分别为 7.7496 元 / 欧元、6.0485 元 /100 日元、8.8144 元 / 英镑、5.2099 元 / 澳元、5.2144 元 / 加元，分别较上年末贬值 5.7%、1.5%、3.5%、3.7% 和 1.4%。

人民币对一篮子货币小幅贬值。根据中国外汇交易中心的数据，2017 年 6 月末 CFETS 人民币汇率指数、参考 BIS 货币篮子和 SDR 货币篮子的人民币汇率指数分别为 93.29、94.25 和 94.18，分别较上年末贬值 1.6%、2.1% 和 1.4%。

根据国际清算银行（BIS）的数据，2017 年上半年人民币名义有效汇率累计贬值 2.3%，扣除通货膨胀因素的实际有效汇率累计贬值 3.3%（见图 4-3）；2005 年人民币汇率形成机制改革以来，人民币名义和实际有效汇率累计分别升值 34.3% 和 42.3%，在 BIS 监测的 61 种货币中分别居第 3 位和第 2 位，人民币从中长期趋势看仍是全球最稳定的货币。

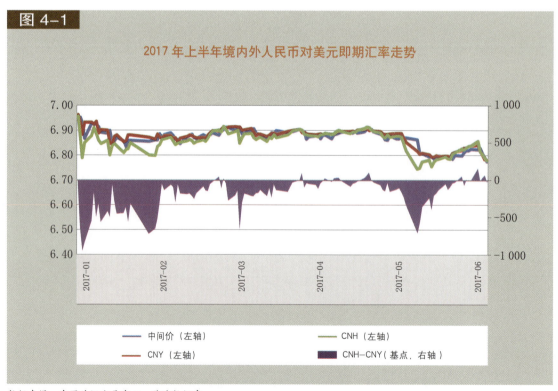

图 4-1

2017 年上半年境内外人民币对美元即期汇率走势

中间价（左轴）　　CNH（左轴）
CNY（左轴）　　CNH-CNY（基点，右轴）

数据来源：中国外汇交易中心，路透数据库。

图 4-2

境内外人民币对美元即期汇率价差

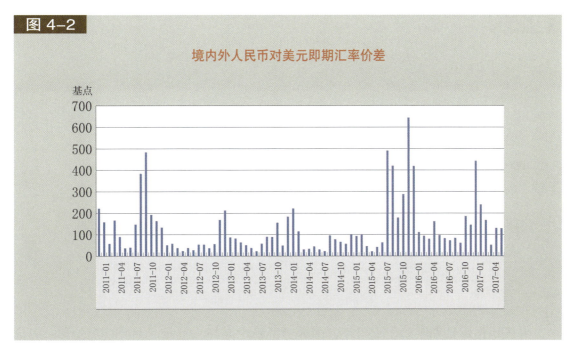

注：日均价差绝对值。
数据来源：中国外汇交易中心，路透数据库。

图 4-3

人民币有效汇率

———— 名义有效汇率　　　　———— 实际有效汇率

数据来源：国际清算银行。

图 4-4

境内外市场人民币对美元汇率 1 年期波动率

数据来源：彭博资讯。

人民币汇率预期平稳。上半年，国内经济稳中向好、美元汇率持续走弱和中间价报价模型引入"逆周期因子"，在内外部市场环境和汇率形成机制层面为人民币汇率保持基本稳定提供了支持。6 月末，境内外市场人民币对美元汇率 1 年期历史波动率分别为 2.6% 和 3.4%，较年初分别下降 6.8% 和 1.8%；期权市场隐含波动率分别为 3.4% 和 4.7%，较年初分别下降 34.8% 和 41.6%（见图 4-4），人民币汇率贬值预期大幅减弱。

远期外汇市场价格走强。上半年，市场非理性和恐慌性购汇情绪缓解，企业远期净购汇回落，加之本外币利差逐步收窄，推动境内外远期外汇市场人民币逐步回升（见图 4-5 和图 4-6）。上半年，境内外可交割和无本金交割远期市场 1 年期人民币对美元汇率累计分别上涨 1.7%、5.3% 和 5.6%。

图 4-5

境内外市场 1 年期人民币对美元汇率

数据来源：中国外汇交易中心，路透数据库。

图 4-6

境内人民币与美元利差（6个月期限）

利差1（人民币shibor–境内美元拆借）　　　利差2–利差1

利差2（外汇掉期隐含）

数据来源：中国外汇交易中心，路透数据库。

（二）外汇市场交易

2017年上半年，人民币外汇市场累计成交10.49万亿美元（日均881亿美元），同比增长17.8%（见图4-7）。其中，银行对客户市场和银行间外汇市场分别成交1.79万亿美元和8.69万亿美元[①]；即期和衍生产品分别成交4.39万亿美元和6.09万亿美元（见表4-1），衍生产品在外汇市场交易总量中的比重升至历史新高的58.1%，交易产品构成进一步接近全球外汇市场状况（见图4-8）。

即期外汇交易平稳增长。 2017年上半年，即期市场累计成交4.39万亿美元，同比增长10.1%。在市场分布上，银行对客户即期结售汇（含银行自身，不含远期履约）累计1.49万亿美元，同比增长2.3%；银行间即期外汇市场累计成交2.90万亿美元，同比增长14.6%，其中美元交易份额为96.3%。

远期外汇交易有所回升。 2017年上半年，远期市场累计成交1 695亿美元，同比增长11.1%。在市场分布上，银行对客户远期结售汇累计签约1 290亿美元，同比增长19.1%，其中结汇693亿美元，增长94.3%，售汇598亿美元，下降17.8%（见

---

① 银行对客户市场采用客户买卖外汇总额，银行间外汇市场采用单边交易量，以下同。

图 4-7

中国外汇市场交易量

数据来源：国家外汇管理局，中国外汇交易中心。

图 4-8

中国与全球外汇市场的交易产品构成比较

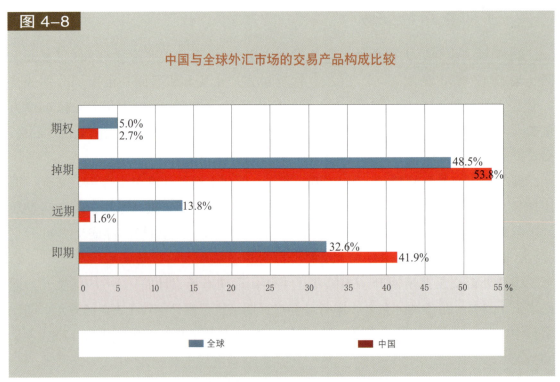

注：中国为2017年上半年数据，全球为国际清算银行2016年4月调查数据。
数据来源：国家外汇管理局，中国外汇交易中心，国际清算银行。

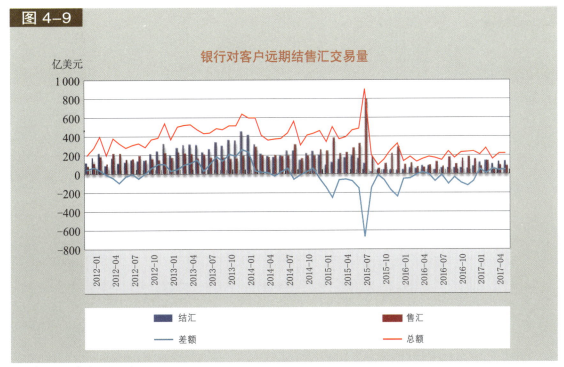

图 4-9

银行对客户远期结售汇交易量

亿美元

结汇　　　售汇
差额　　　总额

数据来源：国家外汇管理局。

图 4-9）；6 个月以内的短期交易占 67.1%，较 2016 年增长 7.8 个百分点；银行间远期外汇市场累计成交 404 亿美元，同比下降 8.5%。

掉期交易延续增长。2017 年上半年，外汇和货币掉期市场累计成交 5.6 万亿美元，同比增长 25.6%。在市场分布上，银行对客户外汇和货币掉期累计签约 506 亿美元，同比下降 6.5%，其中近端结汇 / 远端购汇和近端购汇 / 远端结汇的交易量分别为 381 亿美元和 125 亿美元，同比分别增长 27.9% 和下降 48.7%，主要反映了远期汇率变化对市场主体本外币流动性和融资管理的影响；银行间外汇和货币掉期市场累计成交 5.6 万亿美元，同比增长 26.0%。

外汇期权交易小幅增长。2017 年上半年，期权市场累计成交 2 807 亿美元，同比增长 4.8%。在市场分布上，银行对客户期权市场累计成交 1 214 亿美元，同比增长 44.2%，人民币汇率双向浮动显示出期权交易在汇率风险管理上的灵活性和吸引力；银行间外汇期权市场累计成交 1 593 亿美元，同比下降 13.3%。

外汇市场参与者结构保持稳定。银行自营交易延续主导地位（见图 4-10），2017 年上半年银行间交易占整个外汇市场的比重为 82.3%，非金融客户和非银行金融机构交易的比重分别为 16.9% 和 0.9%，与 2016 年基本持平。

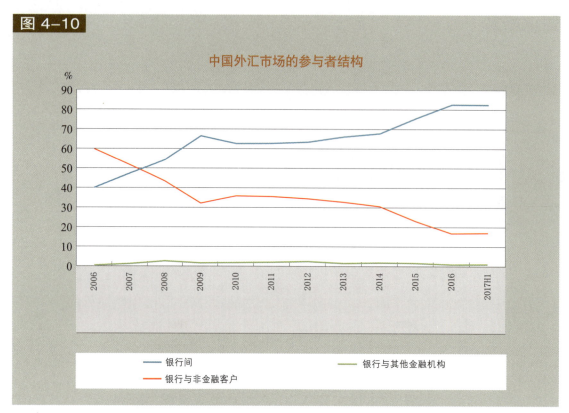

图 4-10

中国外汇市场的参与者结构

图例：
- 银行间
- 银行与非金融客户
- 银行与其他金融机构

数据来源：国家外汇管理局，中国外汇交易中心。

表 4-1　2017 年上半年人民币外汇市场交易概况

交易品种	交易量（亿美元）
即期	43 949
银行对客户市场	14 924
银行间外汇市场	29 025
远期	1 695
银行对客户市场	1 290
其中：3 个月（含）以下	636
3 个月至 1 年（含）	568
1 年以上	87
银行间外汇市场	404
其中：3 个月（含）以下	266
3 个月至 1 年（含）	123
1 年以上	15
外汇和货币掉期	56 412
银行对客户市场	506
银行间外汇市场	55 906
其中：3 个月（含）以下	48 402

续表

交易品种	交易量（亿美元）
3 个月至 1 年（含）	7 451
1 年以上	53
期权	2 807
银行对客户市场	1 214
其中：买入期权	607
卖出期权	607
其中：3 个月（含）以下	281
3 个月至 1 年（含）	758
1 年以上	175
银行间外汇市场	1 593
其中：3 个月（含）以下	1 075
3 个月至 1 年（含）	513
1 年以上	5
合计	104 863
银行对客户市场	17 935
银行间外汇市场	86 928
其中：即期	43 949
远期	1 695
外汇和货币掉期	56 412
期权	2 807

注：数据均为单边交易额，采用四舍五入原则。

数据来源：国家外汇管理局，中国外汇交易中心。

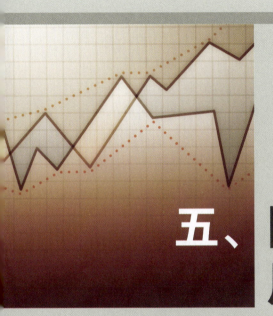

五、国际收支形势展望

2017 年下半年，我国国际收支有望保持基本平衡格局。

经常账户将维持较合理的顺差规模。 第一，货物贸易顺差较上半年将有所扩大。从出口看，全球经济总体延续回稳势头有利于我国外需稳定，国际货币基金组织 2017 年 7 月预测，2017 年和 2018 年全球经济分别增长 3.5% 和 3.6%，快于此前两年的增长水平，其中，发达经济体分别增长 2.0% 和 1.9%，新兴市场和发展中国家分别增长 4.6% 和 4.8%。同时，"一带一路"倡议和国际产能合作等稳步推进有利于促进区域贸易发展，下半年西方重要节日也会季节性拉动出口上升。从进口看，我国经济运行总体稳中向好，主要进口大宗商品价格在经历反弹后可能相对趋稳，进口增速将保持基本稳定。第二，服务贸易逆差增幅总体仍会趋于平稳。旅行项目是当前服务贸易逆差的主要来源，境外旅游、留学等需求在过去两年多时间里得到较快释放，近期已逐步达到较稳定的规模。第三，过去几年我国对外金融资产结构不断优化，官方储备以外的对外投资逐步增加，相关投资收益开始有所体现，这有利于推动我国境外投资收益增长和投资收益逆差收窄。总体来看，预计 2017 年全年经常账户顺差与 GDP 之比仍将处于合理水平。

跨境资本流动仍将保持总体稳定。 未来我国跨境资本流动总体企稳的条件继续存在。第一，国内经济企稳向好的势头更加稳固、更加可持续。2017 年以来，国际货币基金组织多次上调对 2017 年中国经济增速的预测结果，目前预计 2017 年中国经济增长 6.7%，与 2016 年经济增速持平，代表了国际社会的客观判断。第二，国内市场更加开放。例如，近期国家出台了一系列有利于外资的重大举措，随着相关措施逐步落地，外商直接投资仍将保持基本稳定；"债券通"已正式启动、A 股也将纳入明晟新兴市场指数（MSCI），这将逐步对境外投资者投资境内证券市场产生积极作用；全口径跨境融资宏观审慎管理政策也在防范风险的同时，继续便利企业融资。第三，境内主体市场预期和对外资产负债调整更加平稳。当前，人民币汇率形成机制不断完善，境内主体对外投资更趋理性，对外负债平稳恢复，有助于形成形势好转带动市场预期改善，并促进国际收支平衡的良性循环。而且，当前美联储货币政策正常化进程基本符合市场预期，对市场的冲击尤其是对美元汇率的提振作用有所减弱，如果美元汇率保持稳定，将有助于我国跨境资本流动趋稳。当然，宏观经济环境中的不确定性因素依然存在，包括美国、欧洲等经济走势及其货币政策调整对国际汇市的传导效应、贸易保护主义对国际贸易的冲击等，需要实时评估其变化对我国国际收支和跨境资本流动的影响。此外，从长期看，我国经常账户顺差正在合理区间内逐步收窄、对内和对外直接投资呈现此消彼长的发展态势，这些变化对我国国际收支结构和平衡的影响也需持续关注。

2017 年下半年，外汇管理部门将按照党中央、国务院的统一部署，继续贯彻落实全国金融工作会议精神，紧紧围绕服务实体经济、防控金融风险、深化金融改革三项任务开展工作。一方面，坚持改革开放，完善外汇政策框架，支持和推动金融市场的双向开放，审慎有序推动资本项目可兑换，提升跨境贸易和投资便利化水平，服务实体经济；另一方面，防范跨境资本流动风险，构建跨境资本流动的宏观审慎管理和微观市场监管体系，维护外汇市场稳定，为改革开放创造健康良性稳定的市场环境。

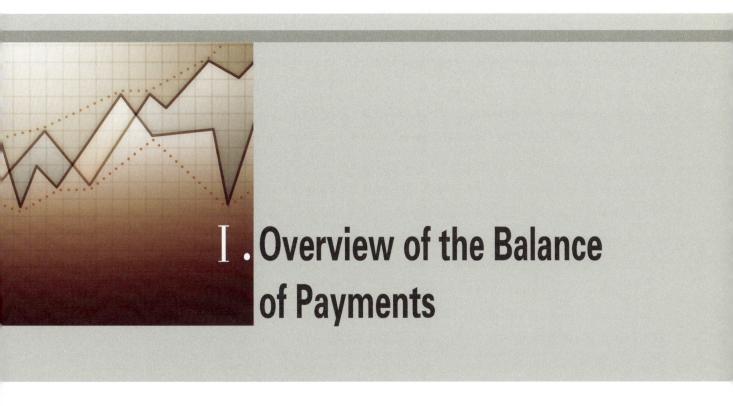

I. Overview of the Balance
of Payments

(I) The Balance—of—Payments Environment

During the first half of 2017, both domestically and externally China faced an improved BOP environment. Although the profound influence of the international financial crisis still existed, the global economy was continuing its steady recovery, thereby creating a stable external environment. The domestic economy was even more positive.

In general, the global economy recovered steadily. During the first half of the year, the global economy was recovering. The IMF and the OECD successively adjusted their expectations about global economic growth to 3.5 percent in 2017, and the performance of the major economies was diversified (see Chart 1–1). The recovery in the United States was characterized by twists and turns. Its economic growth revealed an upward trend with fluctuations and the unemployment rate remained low, but the progress of the fiscal stimulus was slower than expected, which undercut economic expectations. Political uncertainties in the Euro zone declined and the economic fundamentals continued to improve, but the momentum of inflation was still insufficient. Japan was building a momentum for recovery, and its economic growth recorded its best performance since the international financial crisis, and inflation was also tending to rebound. The emerging economies were growing rapidly, although some economies still faced adjustment and transformation pressures.Against the background that global demand was growing slowly and the monetary policies of the advanced economies might be adjusted, there were potential risks of weak external demand and of fluctuations in cross—border capital flows.

The monetary policies of the developed economies and the emerging economies became diversified. The major advanced economies were considering embarking on a process of monetary—policy normalization. During the first half of the year, the Fed increased the target of the federal funds rate by 25 basis points on two occasions respectively to a range of 1 percent to 1.25 percent, and it maintained its expectation that it would raise the federal funds rate once again in 2017 and three times in 2018. The Fed also proposed a target to normalize its balance sheet. The ECB decided to keep its key interest rate and asset purchasing plan unchanged, which clearly indicated that the risks of deflation had diminished. The Bank of Japan announced on four occasions that it would maintain the original negative interest rates and the original volume of asset purchases. However, at the same time it began to discuss the withdrawal of its quantitative easing policy. The monetary policies of the emerging economies were also diversifying. Some economies, such as Russia and Brazil, further eased their monetary policies to promote economic growth. But other economies, including Mexico, raised

Chart 1–1

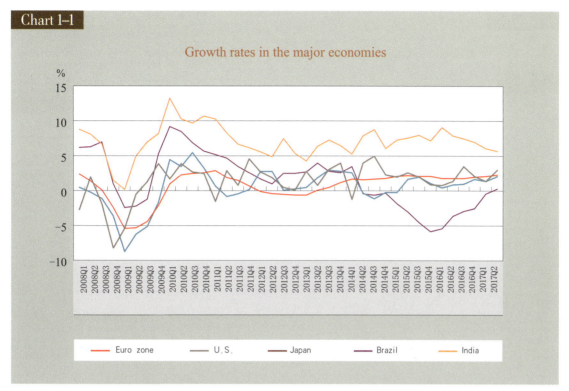

Growth rates in the major economies

Note: The US growth rate is the annualized quarterly growth rate; the growth rates of the other countries are the year-on-year quarterly growth rates.
Source: CEIC.

their benchmark interest rates against exchange–rate depreciations, capital outflows, and inflationary pressures.

A decline in fluctuations in the international financial market. Backed up by the steady recovery of the global economy, fluctuations in the international financial market generally decreased. During the first half of the year, the USD weakened, the Euro, the Sterling, and the Japanese Yen appreciated significantly against the USD, and the USD index was down by 6.4 percent. The currencies of the emerging markets experienced ups and downs and the EMCI by JP Morgan appreciated by 4.1 percent. During the first half of the year, market risk aversions were alleviated. Global stock markets recorded a general rise and commodity prices rose slightly. The VIX decreased by 20.4 percent, and the Dow Jones Industrial Average Index, the Euro STOXX50, and the MSCI Emerging Market Index rose by 8.0 percent, 8.2 percent, and 17.2 percent respectively. The S&P GSCI rose by 4.6 percent (see Chart 1–2 and Chart1–3). In the future, the normalization of the monetary policies of the major economies, de–globalization, trade protectionism, and related risks of geopolitical conflicts will continue to challenge global economic and financial stability.

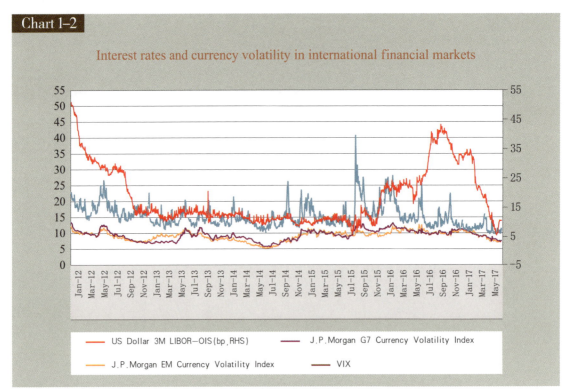

Chart 1–2

Interest rates and currency volatility in international financial markets

— US Dollar 3M LIBOR—OIS (bp, RHS)   — J.P.Morgan G7 Currency Volatility Index

— J.P.Morgan EM Currency Volatility Index   — VIX

Source: Bloomberg.

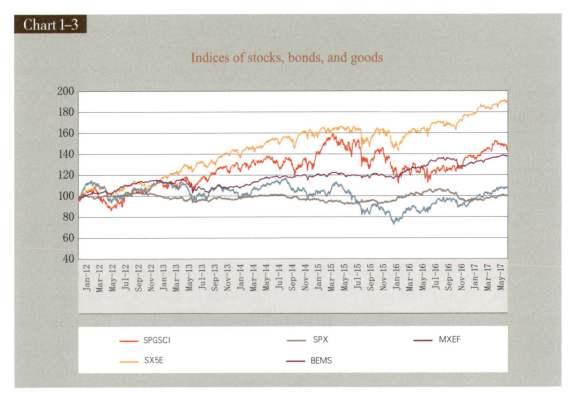

Chart 1–3

Indices of stocks, bonds, and goods

— SPGSCI   — SPX   — MXEF

— SX5E   — BEMS

Note: BEMS refers to the Bloomberg Emerging Markets Sovereign Bond Index; BGSV refers to the Bloomberg Advanced Countries Sovereign Bond Index; MXEF refers to the MSCI Emerging Markets Index; SPX refers to Standard & Poor's 500 Index; SX5E refers to the Euro STOXX50 Index; and SPGSCI refers to Standard & Poor's GSCI Index. 2012=100.
Source: Bloomberg.

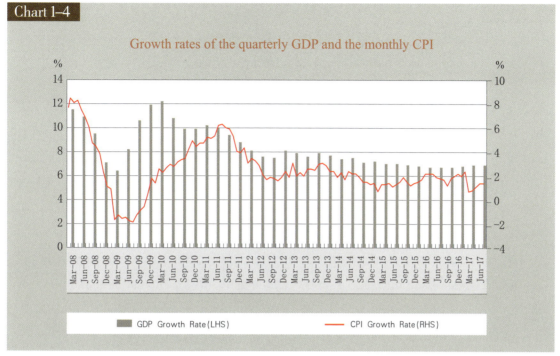

Chart 1–4

Growth rates of the quarterly GDP and the monthly CPI

GDP Growth Rate (LHS) — CPI Growth Rate (RHS)

Source: NBS.

The domestic economy registered increasingly stable performance, with a good momentum for growth. In the first half of the year, China's economic performance was stable, along with the further supply–side structural reforms and the more rapid transformation and upgrading. Economic growth was strongly stimulated by consumption demand, and investments and exports/imports maintained strong growth, which led to strengthened stability, coordination, and sustainability of economic growth. During the first half of the year, GDP totaled USD 38.15 trillion, up by 6.9 percent year on year; the CPI rose by 1.4 percent (see Chart 1–4); the employment situation was steady and improving; the proportion of the contribution of tertiary industry to GDP increased by 54.1 percent; and the final contribution of consumer spending to the GDP growth rate was 63.4 percent. However, China's economic growth was more or less driven by the strengthened external demand due to the global economic recovery. The momentum for internal growth should be further strengthened and structural conflicts should be gradually resolved.

Box 1

Normalization of the Fed monetary policy

In June 2017, the FOMC meeting decided to increase the target of the federal funds rate by 25 basis points on two occasions respectively to a range of 1 percent to 1.25 percent, and stated that before year-end the Fed would begin to reduce its balance sheet. The addendum of the statement clarified that the Fed would gradually and predictably reduce the size of its balance sheet by decreasing its reinvestments of the principal payments it receives from securities held in the System Open Market Account. The initial cap would be USD 6 billion for Treasury securities and USD 4 billion for MBSs, and there after the cap would be increased in stages of USD 6 billion and USD 4 billion at 3-month intervals until it reached USD 30 billion and USD 20 billion respectively. As Chair Yellen said, the purpose of publicly announcing the plan to reduce the balance sheet was to alleviate market tensions. The plan was to be implemented as soon as possible, and it would be properly adjusted in accord with a deterioration in the economic situation. In September, the FOMC meeting decided to keep the target rate unchanged and it stated that the Fed would begin the process of reducing the balance sheet in October and would once again raise the target rate in 2017.

The Fed benefits from the current economic and market environments to maintain its plan to raise the target rate on three occasions and to begin reducing its balance sheet in 2017. The United States is very close to sufficient employment, as its unemployment rate is 4.3 percent, lower than the NAIRU estimated by the Fed. According to traditional economic theory, the economy is overheated, which has led to concerns that the pace of raising the target rate is insufficient. In addition, the current interest rate is low, and could possibly reach a floor of zero if there were to be a financial crisis. An early tightening will provide room for more policy space in the future. However, raising the rate without reducing the balance sheet may lead to a tightening imbalance because a rise in therate will increase the short-term rate, but maintaining a large balance sheet will place downward pressures on mid-and long-term interest rates, which together will distort the interest rate curve. Hence, a reduction in the balance sheet will be conducive to monetary-policy normalization after arise in the interest rate. Beginning in the second half of 2016, the economic indicatorsin both the United States andthe global economy recorded an improving trend, and external risks, such the French elections, diminished, which provided an appropriate window to raise the interest rate and to reduce the balance sheet.

Although the recent weak inflation deviated from the expectations of both the Fedand the market, the target of normalizing monetary policy cannot be easily adjusted. First, the momentum for endogenous growth is firm. The steady growth of employment, the historically–highwealth, and the strong confidence indicate stable growth of consumption. In terms of investments, because oil prices have dropped to a reasonable range, the global economy has continued to recover, and the drag from the strong USD has been alleviated, industrial output and investments by enterprises will grow moderately. Second, the mid–term inflation is expected to grow slowly. The inflation rate recently declined due to short–term factors such as the fall in oil and electricity prices. Since the economic recovery has been sustained, the inflation rate is approaching the Fed's target of 2 percent. Third, financial conditions have eased. Since December 2016, although the Fed raised its rate on three occasions and published its plan to reduce the balance sheet, the yields of long–term treasury bonds and of the US Dollar Index decreased with fluctuations and the stock market recorded a historical high, which provided the Fed with room to further tighten monetary policy and made the Fed more cautious regarding asset bubbles.

The effects of the Fed's tightening of monetary policy on the emerging markets require continued attention. Historical experience shows that if the Fed raises its rate more rapidly than expected, the market rate will rise significantly, which will lead to capital out flows in the emerging markets. China, as the largest emerging economy, will inevitably face pressures of capital outflows. Thus far, the normalization of the Fed's monetary policy has been stable and the economic fundamentals have been key to preventing risks. China has been safely buffered from changes in the external environment by its steadily improving macro economic performance, its sustained current account surplus, its controllable external debt, and its sufficient foreign reserves at about USD 3 trillion.

(II) The Main Characteristics of the Balance of Payments

During the first half of the year, both the current account and the non–reserve financial account recorded a surplus, of USD 69.3 billion and USD 67.9 billion respectively, which is called a BOP twin surplus (see Table 1–1).

Table 1-1 Structure of the BOP surplus

BOP balance	2011	2012	2013	2014	2015	2016	2016H1	2017H1
Current account balance	1 361	2 154	1 482	2 360	3 042	1 964	1 103	693
As a % of the BOP balance	1.8%	2.5%	1.5%	2.3%	2.7%	1.8%	2.1%	1.2%
Capital and financial account balance	2 600	-360	3 430	-514	-4 345	-4 170	-1 787	679
As a % of GDP	3.4%	-0.4%	3.6%	-0.5%	-3.9%	-3.7%	-3.4%	1.2%

Sources: SAFE, NBS.

The surplus of trade in goods continued. Based on the balance–of–payments statistics, [①]during the first half of 2017 exports and imports of trade in goods totaled USD 1026.9 billion and USD 812.6 billion respectively, up by 12 percent and 18 percent. The surplus totaled USD 214.4

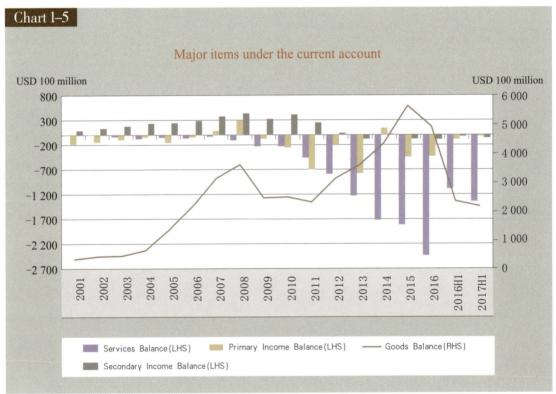

Chart 1–5

Major items under the current account

Source: SAFE.

---

① The BOP statistics and the statistics of the General Administration of Customs with respect to trade in goods can be reconciled by the following: First, trade in goods in the BOP records transactions when the transfer of the ownership of goods (such as ordinary trade and processing trade goods with imported materials) and transactions without ownership transfers (such as processing trade with customers' materials and outward processing) are regarded as trade in services instead of trade in goods. Second, the BOP records imports and exports based on FOB, whereas the General Administration of Customs records exports based on FOB but it records imports based on CIF. Thus, the BOP statistics deduct insurance and freight from the value of imports and add them to the trade in services. Third, information on repatriations is included. Fourth, net exports of goods under the turnover of goods, which are collected by the General Administration of Customs, are also included.

billion, down by 8 percent (see Chart 1–5).

The trade-in-services deficit continued.[1]During the first half of the year, revenue and expenditures in trade in services totaled USD 101.4 billion and USD 236.4 billion respectively, up by 0.4 percent and 13 percent year on year. Trade in services posted a deficit of USD 135.1 billion, up by 24 percent. In particular, the deficit in transportation totaled USD 26.2 billion, up by 26 percent. and the deficit in travel totaled USD 115.9 billion, up by 19 percent (see Chart 1–5).

The deficit in primary income decreased. During the first half of the year, revenue and expenditures of primary income totaled USD 125 billion and USD 128.4 billion respectively, up by 15 percent and 9 percent. Primary income recorded a deficit of USD 3.4 billion, down by 65 percent. In particular, employee compensation recorded a surplus of USD 8.5 billion, down by 21 percent. Investment income recorded a deficit of USD 12.2 billion, down by 41 percent (see Chart 1–5). In terms of investment income, outward investment income totaled USD 113 billion, up by 19 percent, and inward investment expenditures, including profits, interest, and dividends, totaled USD 125.2 billion, up by 9 percent.

The deficit in secondary income increased. During the first half of the year, secondary–income revenue totaled USD 14.7 billion, down by 9 percent. Secondary–income expenditures totaled USD 21.3 billion, up by 9 percent. The deficit in secondary income was USD 6.7 billion, up by 99 percent (see Chart 1–5).

Direct investments turned to a surplus. Based on the BOP statistics,[2] direct investments posted a surplus of USD 13.9 billion, whereas in the first half of 2016 they recorded a deficit of USD 49.4 billion (see Chart 1–6). In particular, the net increase in direct–investment assets totaled USD 41.1 billion, down by 67 percent, and the net increase in direct–investment liabilities totaled USD 55 billion, down by 26 percent.

The deficit in portfolio investments decreased. During the first half of the year, the deficit in portfolio investments totaled USD 19.5 billion, down by 41 percent year on year (see Chart 1–6). In particular, the net outflow of outward portfolio investments (a net increase in assets) totaled USD 40.1 billion, up by 6 percent, and the net inflow of inward portfolio investments (a net increase of liabilities) totaled USD 20.6 billion, up by 3.5 times.

---

[1] The IMF's *Balance of Payments and International Investment Manual* (sixth edition) renamed the income item under the current account as primary income and renamed current transfers as secondary income.

[2] Unlike the data released by the Ministry of Commerce, direct investments based on the BOP statistics also include unpaid and unremitted profits, retained earnings, shareholder loans, foreign capital utilized by financial institutions, and real estate purchases by non–residents.

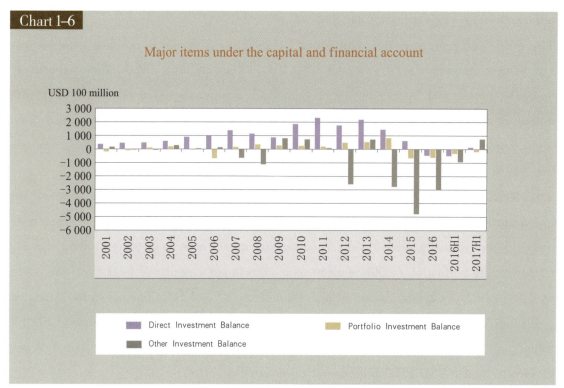

Chart 1–6

Major items under the capital and financial account

USD 100 million

Source: SAFE.

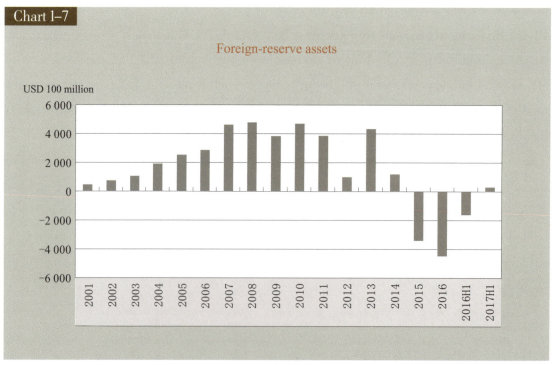

Chart 1–7

Foreign-reserve assets

USD 100 million

Source: SAFE.

Other investments recorded a surplus. During the first half of the year, other investments, including loans, trade credits, and deposits, recorded a surplus of USD 73.2 billion, whereas in the first half of 2016 they had recorded a deficit of USD 93.8 billion (see Chart 1–6). In particular, net outflows of outward other investments (a net increase in assets) totaled USD 53.6 billion, down by 29 percent, and net inflows of inward other investments (a net increase of liabilities) totaled USD 126.7 billion, whereas during the first half of 2016 they recorded a net outflow of USD 17.9 billion.

An increase in reserve assets. During the first half of 2017, reserve assets involving transactions (excluding the effects of non–transactional values, such as the exchange rate and prices) increased by USD 29 billion. In particular, foreign–reserve assets involving transactions increased by USD 29.4 billion (see Chart 1–7). By the end of June 2017, China's foreign–reserve assets totaled USD 3056.8 billion, up by USD 46.3 billion from the end of 2016.

Table 1-2 Balance of payments in 2017H1

Unit: USD 100 million

Item	Line No.	2017H1
1. Current account	1	693
Credit	2	12 680
Debit	3	-11 987
1.A Goods and services	4	793
Credit	5	11 283
Debit	6	-10 490
1.A.a Goods	7	2 144
Credit	8	10 269
Debit	9	-8 126
1.A.b Services	10	-1 351
Credit	11	1 014
Debit	12	-2 364
1.A.b.1 Manufacturing services on physical inputs owned by others	13	87
Credit	14	88
Debit	15	-1
1.A.b.2 Maintenance and repair services n.i.e	16	18
Credit	17	28
Debit	18	-10
1.A.b.3 Transport	19	-262
Credit	20	173
Debit	21	-435
1.A.b.4 Travel	22	-1 159
Credit	23	188
Debit	24	-1 347
1.A.b.5 Construction	25	10
Credit	26	53
Debit	27	-42
1.A.b.6 Insurance and pension services	28	-33
Credit	29	18
Debit	30	-51
1.A.b.7 Financial services	31	8
Credit	32	14

70

(Continued)

Item	Line No.	2017H1
Debit	33	-7
1.A.b.8 Charges for the use of intellectual property	34	-121
Credit	35	22
Debit	36	-143
1.A.b.9 Telecommunications, computer, and information services	37	45
Credit	38	136
Debit	39	-91
1.A.b.10 Other business services	40	76
Credit	41	282
Debit	42	-206
1.A.b.11 Personal, cultural, and recreational services	43	-9
Credit	44	4
Debit	45	-12
1.A.b.12 Government goods and services n.i.e	46	-11
Credit	47	8
Debit	48	-19
1.B Primary income	49	-34
Credit	50	1 250
Debit	51	-1 284
1.B.1 Compensation of employees	52	85
Credit	53	117
Debit	54	-32
1.B.2 Investment income	55	-122
Credit	56	1 130
Debit	57	-1 252
1.B.3 Other primary income	58	2
Credit	59	3
Debit	60	-1
1.C Secondary income	61	-67
Credit	62	147
Debit	63	-213
2. Capital and financial account	64	389
2.1 Capital account	65	-1
Credit	66	1
Debit	67	-2
2.2 Financial account	68	390
Assets	69	-1 632
Liabilities	70	2 021
2.2.1 Financial account excluding reserve assets	71	679
Financial assets excluding reserve assets	72	-1 342
Liabilities	73	2 021
2.2.1.1 Direct investment	74	139
2.2.1.1.1 Assets	75	-411
2.2.1.1.1.1 Equity and investment fund shares	76	-419
2.2.1.1.1.2 Debt instruments	77	8
2.2.1.1.2 Liabilities	78	550
2.2.1.1.2.1 Equity and investment fund shares	79	520
2.2.1.1.2.2 Debt instruments	80	30
2.2.1.2 Portfolio investment	81	-195
2.2.1.2.1 Assets	82	-401
2.2.1.2.1.1 Equity and investment fund shares	83	-142
2.2.1.2.1.2 Debt securities	84	-259
2.2.1.2.2 Liabilities	85	206

(Continued)

Item	Line No.	2017H1
2.2.1.2.2.1 Equity and investment fund shares	86	116
2.2.1.2.2.2 Debt securities	87	90
2.2.1.3 Financial derivatives (other than reserves) and employee stock options	88	3
2.2.1.3.1 Assets	89	5
2.2.1.3.2 Liabilities	90	-2
2.2.1.4 Other investment	91	732
2.2.1.4.1 Assets	92	-536
2.2.1.4.1.1 Other equity	93	-1
2.2.1.4.1.2 Currency and deposits	94	-83
2.2.1.4.1.3 Loans	95	-665
2.2.1.4.1.4 Insurance, pension, and standardized guarantee schemes	96	-3
2.2.1.4.1.5 Trade credit and advances	97	296
2.2.1.4.1.6 Other accounts receivable	98	-80
2.2.1.4.2 Liabilities	99	1 267
2.2.1.4.2.1 Other equity	100	0
2.2.1.4.2.2 Currency and deposits	101	995
2.2.1.4.2.3 Loans	102	547
2.2.1.4.2.4 Insurance, pension, and standardized guarantee schemes	103	2
2.2.1.4.2.5 Trade credit and advances	104	-339
2.2.1.4.2.6 Other accounts payable	105	62
2.2.1.4.2.7 Special drawing rights	106	0
2.2.2 Reserve assets	107	-290
2.2.2.1 Monetary gold	108	0
2.2.2.2 Special drawing rights	109	0
2.2.2.3 Reserve position in the IMF	110	4
2.2.2.4 Foreign exchange reserves	111	-294
2.2.2.5 Other reserve assets	112	0
3.Net errors and omissions	113	-1 081

Notes:
1. This chart was compiled according to the Balance of Payments Manual (sixth edition).
2. In the financial account, a positive value for assets indicates a net decrease, whereas a negative value indicates a net increase. A positive value for liabilities indicates a net increase, whereas a negative value indicates a net decrease.
3. The chart is based on a rounding principle.
Source: SAFE.

(III) Evaluation of the Balance of Payments

The current account surplus was reasonable. During the first half of 2017, the ratio of the current account surplus to GDP was 1.2 percent, which was considered reasonable. In particular, the ratio was 0.7 percent and 1.7 percent during the first and second quarters respectively. In terms of the items, the ratio of the balance of trade in goods to GDP was 3.9 percent, the ratio of the balance of trade in services to GDP was–2.4 percent, and the ratio of the balance of primary income and secondary income to GDP was–0.2 percent (see Chart 1–8).

Cross-border capital flows steadily recovered. During the first half of the year, the non–reserve financial account recorded a surplus of USD 67.9 billion, whereas in the first half year of 2016 it had recorded a deficit of USD 178.7 billion. Beginning in the second quarter of 2014, the non–reserve financial account posted deficits for eleven consecutive quarters

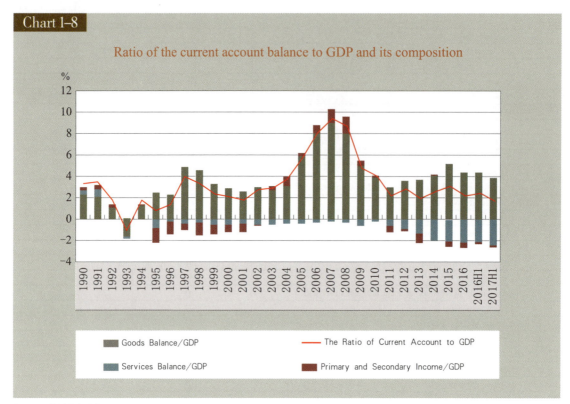

Chart 1–8

Ratio of the current account balance to GDP and its composition

Sources: SAFE, NBS.

until the first quarter of 2017, when it recorded a surplus of USD 36.8 billion. The surplus in the second quarter of 2017 was USD 31.1 billion. Hence, during the first half of the year foreign–reserve assets involving transactions rose steadily and China's balance of payments automatically achieved a better equilibrium (see Chart 1–9).

Outward investments were more rational. During the first half of the year, the net increase of external assets, including outward direct investments, portfolio investments, and other investments, totaled USD 134.2 billion, down by 45 percent year on year. In particular, it totaled USD 54.7 billion and USD 79.5 billion respectively during the first and second quarters. First, outward investments became more rational. During the first half of the year, the net increase in direct–investment assets totaled USD 41.4 billion, down by 67 percent year on year. Although the volume remained high, irrational outward investments were effectively curbed and rational outward investments were strongly supported. Second, outward portfolio investments grew steadily. The net increase in external stock and bond assets totaled USD 40.1 billion, up by 6 percent year on year. In addition, the net increase in other–investment assets totaled USD 53.6 billion, down by 29 percent.

Inward investments rebounded rapidly. During the first half of the year, inward

Chart 1–9

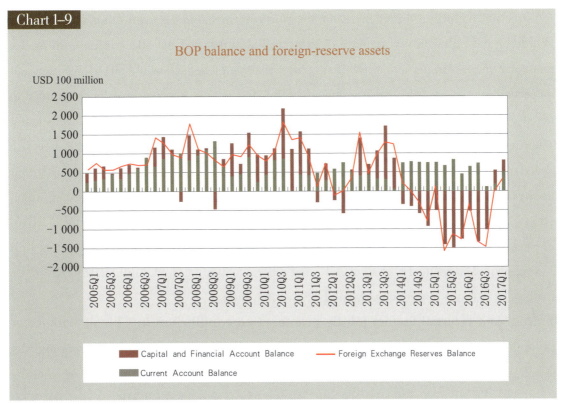

Source: SAFE.

Chart 1–10

The structure of cross-border capital flows in 2016

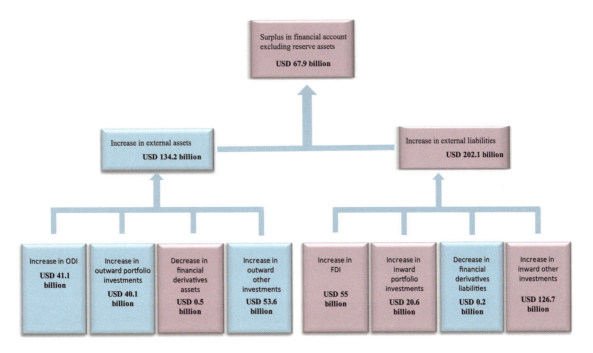

Source: SAFE.

investments, including direct investments, portfolio investments, and other investments, recorded a net inflow (a net increase of external liabilities) of USD 202.1 billion, up by 2.2 times year on year. In particular, the first quarter recorded a net inflow of USD 91.5 billion and the second quarter recorded a net inflow of USD 110.6 billion. Foreign investors continued to increase their investments in China. The direct–investment item recorded a net foreign–capital inflow of USD 55 billion. In addition, with the deepening of the opening up of the domestic capital market, the net inflow of inward portfolio investments totaled USD 20.6 billion, up by 3.5 times year on year. However, domestic entities were more willing to finance from abroad, which led to a rise in demand for cross–border financing. Beginning in the second quarter of 2016, external loans by domestic entities recorded a net inflow during five consecutive quarters with a rising scale. During the first half of 2017, net inflows totaled USD 54.7 billion, whereas in the first half of 2016 net outflows had totaled USD 31.8 billion.

Internal and external factors jointly promoted an equilibrium in China's balance of payments. First, on the domestic side the Chinese economy was steadily growing and the global growth rate remained high. Many economic indicators continued to improve, thereby encouraging market confidence. Second, the exchange rate of the RMB against the USD

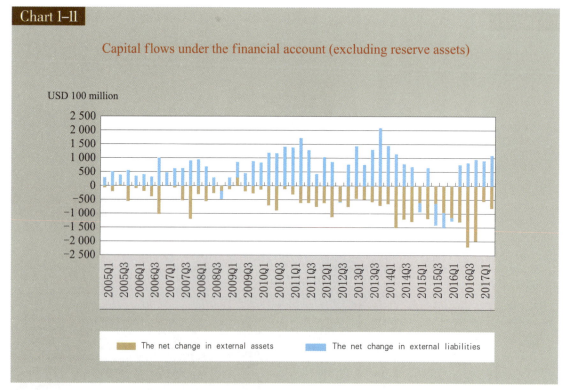

Chart 1–11

Capital flows under the financial account (excluding reserve assets)

USD 100 million

The net change in external assets   The net change in external liabilities

Source: SAFE.

experienced stronger two–way fluctuations. With the improved RMB central parity mechanism, counter–cyclical adjustments became effective, and the expectations of market participants were stabilized, thus helping to steady related purchases and remittances of foreign exchange. Third, as the domestic market became more open, foreign investors became more confident and active in the Chinese market. On the external side, international financial markets were relatively stable, the impact of the shocks from the raising of the rate by the Fed gradually weakened and market participants adapted to the related impacts. In general, the foundation for China's BOP equilibrium became more solid.

Box 2

China achieved steady BOP performance under the status of the new normal

In recent years China has been facing changing economic and financial environments both domestically and externally. Economic growth has been diversified globally. The advanced economies recovered slowly, the growth rate in the emerging economies was declining, and there was a shift in the monetary policy of the advanced economies, which significantly influenced the international financial market. Meanwhile, domestic economic development was facing anew normal. After the 18th National Congress of the Communist Party of China (CPC), in the face of the sophisticated domestic and external environments, the CPC Central Committee, with Comrade Xi Jinping as the core, meticulously examined the situation and endeavored to make innovations, thus achieving reasonable economic performance and promoting supply–side structural reforms, which ushered in a new phase in China's opening–up. In addition, actions were taken to actively guard against the risks of cross–border capital flows, laying a solid foundation against external shocks and for a general equilibrium.

The current account surplus was reasonable and more balanced, indicating an optimized domestic economic structure. During the recent decade, China's current account has gradually reached an equilibrium when measured by the ratio of the surplus in the current account to GDP, which fell from nearly 10 percent in 2007 to a long–term reasonable level of less than 4 percent in 2010. The average ratio of the surplus in the current account to GDP was 2.1 percent from 2013 to 2016;it was 1.2 percent during the first half of 2017 and thus more balanced than prior to 2012. The 18th National Congress of the CPC suggested that economic development should place more reliance on domestic demand, especially consumption demand. From 2013 to 2016,the average annual contribution of final consumption expenditures to China's economic growth was 55 percent, revealing a trend of overall steady growth. During the first half of 2017, the contribution ratio was 63 percent. Strengthened consumption will lead to a decreased savings rate, thus helping to reduce the savings–investment gap (as well as the current account balance, see Chart C2–1). Specifically, the item of trade in goods continued to post a surplus, although imports, driven by domestic demand, grew relatively rapidly and the balance decreased. The deficit in trade in services, especially travel, rose rapidly due to increased personal income, simplified visa policies, and surging outbound travel and study. In 2016, outbound visitors and students totaled 135 million and 0.54 million respectively, 1.6 and 1.4 times the level in 2012.

Chart C2-1 The contribution of consumption to growth and the ratio of the balance in the current account to GDP

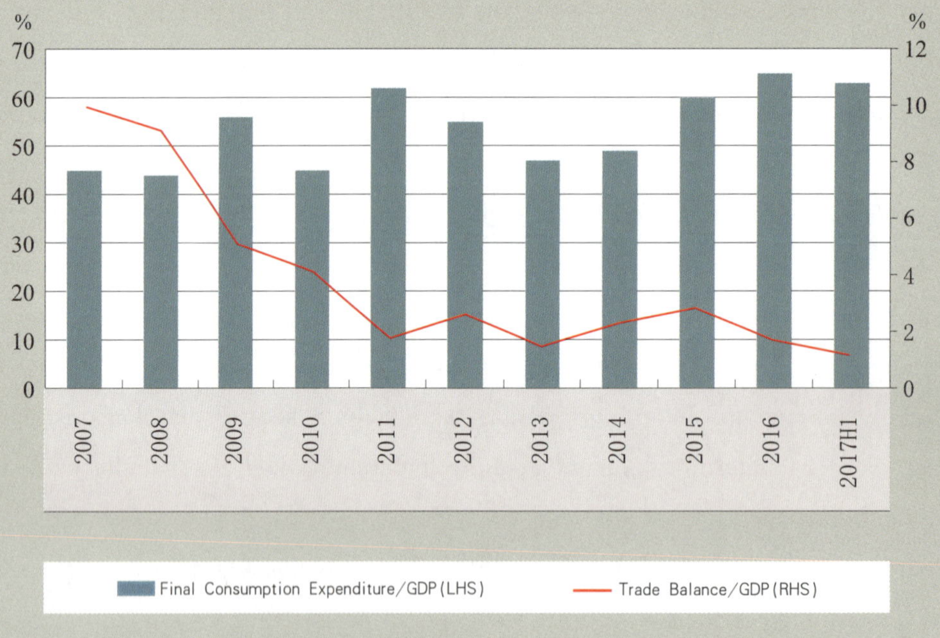

Final Consumption Expenditure/GDP (LHS)   Trade Balance/GDP (RHS)

Sources: NBS, SAFE.

Cross-border capital flows tended to be stable with two-way fluctuations and they effectively responded to adjustments in the external environment. In 2013, China's non–reserve financial account recorded a surplus of USD 343 billion, in 2014 it recorded a small deficit of USD 51.4 billion, and in both 2015 and 2016 it posted a deficit of more than USD 400 billion. During the first half of the year, a surplus of USD 67.9 billion was posted. On the one hand, China's outward direct investments, portfolio investments, and other investments all grew rapidly. This trend was adjusted in 2017 when domestic entities became more rational. On the other hand, inward direct investments remained stable, and the external debt rebounded after a period of deleveraging. The adjustment in China's cross–border capital flows was strongly affected by both the international environment and domestic fundamentals. After the 2008 international financial crisis, the major advanced economies adopted an extremely loose monetary policy, and the emerging economies, including China, faced capital–inflow pressures. However, beginning in 2014 the international environment changed dramatically. The Fed exited from its quantitative easing monetary policy and began to raise interest rates, and some emerging economies faced domestic economic and political issues, which together resulted in outward capital flows from the emerging economies. Under the sophisticated international background, the Central Committee of the CPC and the State Council maintained the goals of steady development and domestic economic and social stability and guarded against regional and systemic risks, providing a solid foundation for more stable cross–border capital flows.

BOP risks were generally controllable, and the structure of external assets and liabilities was improved. China maintained strong international solvency with a low BOP payment risk, a continued current account surplus, and sufficient foreign reserves. Its outstanding foreign reserves are sufficient for over 20 months of imports, which is far higher than the international threshold of 3 or 4 months of imports. It is also over three times the short–term external debt denominated in foreign currency, far higher than the threshold of 100 percent. In addition, the overall risks of external debt are controllable. During the recent five years, the outstanding external debt experienced a process of decreasing and recovering, which helped to release debt–payment pressures. By the end of the second quarter of 2017, the overall outstanding external debt had grown for five consecutive quarters, which was still lower than the historical high at the end of 2014. The external debt/GDP ratio, the external debt/export revenue ratio, and the debt servicing ratio were all below the international threshold. Moreover, the ratio of external assets held by the private sector to total external assets increased from 35 percent at the end of 2012 to 53 percent at the end of the second quarter of 2017, which indicated a better match of external assets and liabilities against related risks. By the end of second of 2017, net external liabilities held by the private sector totaled USD 1.4 trillion, down by USD 122.5 billion from the level at the end of 2012.

In the future, the foundation for economic and social development will be solid with the further opening up of the domestic market and stable cross-border transactions, thus promoting a more balanced situation in terms of the BOP.

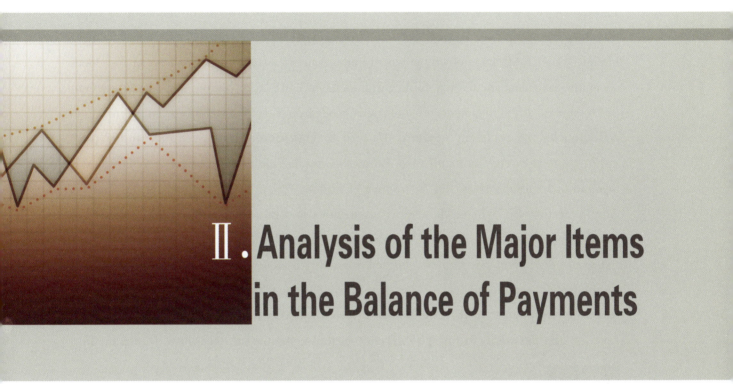

II. Analysis of the Major Items in the Balance of Payments

(I) Trade in goods

Exports and imports of trade in goods recovered and dependence on foreign trade increased slightly. According to the statistics of the General Administration of Customs, in the first half of 2017 exports and imports of trade in goods totaled USD 1.9 trillion, up by 13 percent year on year, and foreign– trade dependence (the ratio of foreign trade to GDP) was 34 percent, up by 2 percentage points (see Chart 2–1), reflecting the fact that China's foreign–trade growth had helped the global trade recovery as well as the recovery of the global economic situation. The foreign–trade surplus totaled USD 183.3 billion, down by 24 percent due to an increase in the import price of staple goods because of the steady economic growth.

Affected by the recovery of domestic and foreign demand, the import and export volume and the price index all rose. Duringthe first half of the year, the recovery of external demand drove up the price and the volume of exports. According to statistics of the General Administration of Customs, the export price index and the export volume index recorded monthly increases of 5 percent and 9 percent respectively. In the meantime, the import volume index and the import price index recorded a monthly increase of 12 percent and 13 percent respectively due to the surge in economic growth and the rise in the price of staple goods.

Revenue and payments of trade in goods posted a decreasing surplus, among which the revenue and payments in foreign currency posted a significant net inflow. During the first

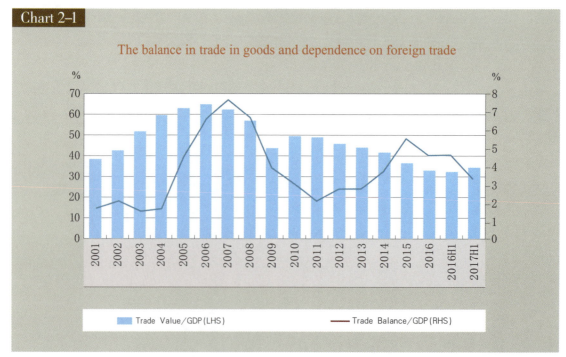

Chart 2–1

The balance in trade in goods and dependence on foreign trade

Trade Value/GDP (LHS)   Trade Balance/GDP (RHS)

Sources: General Administration of Customs, NBS.

Chart 2–2

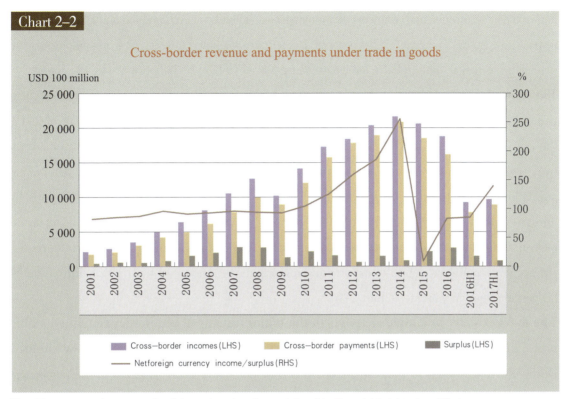

Cross-border revenue and payments under trade in goods

Note: The revenue and payments of trade in goods are based on statistics of the General Administration of Customs.
Source: SAFE.

Chart 2–3

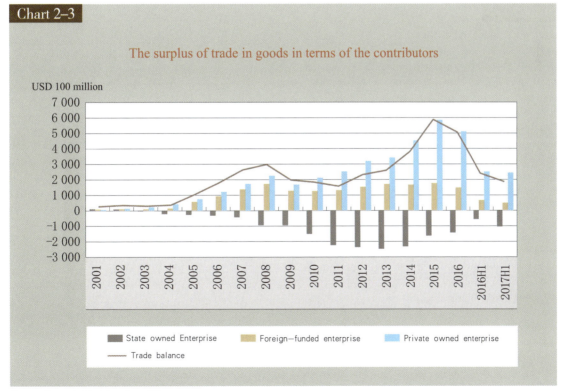

The surplus of trade in goods in terms of the contributors

Source: General Administration of Customs.

half of the year, revenue and payments of trade in goods totaled USD 965.5 billion and USD 886 billion respectively, up by 5 percent and 14 percent. The surplus amounted to USD 79.4 billion, down by 46 percent. In particular, the surplus in foreign exchange totaled USD 112.8 billion, down by 12 percent.

The contribution of the surplus of exports and imports by private enterprises rose and the contribution of foreign-funded enterprises declined slightly. In the first half of 2017, the surplus of exports and imports by private enterprises totaled USD 242.8 billion, down by 3 percent year on year and accounting for 131 percent of the total surplus, 34 percentage points higher than the ratio during the first half of 2016. The surplus of exports and imports by foreign–funded enterprises totaled USD 48.7 billion, down by 26 percent and accounting for 26 percent of the total, the same ratio as that during the first half of 2016. In addition, state–owned enterprises recorded a deficit of exports and imports in the amount of USD 106.5 billion, up by 82 percent year on year (see Chart 2–3).

The market share of Chinaʼs exports to the major advanced economies remained stable and Chinaʼs exports and imports to some"one belt one road"countries grew rapidly. During the first half of the year, China contributed 20 percent of US imports, up by 0.2 percentage point year on year. The market share of imports in the European Union and Japan was 19 percent

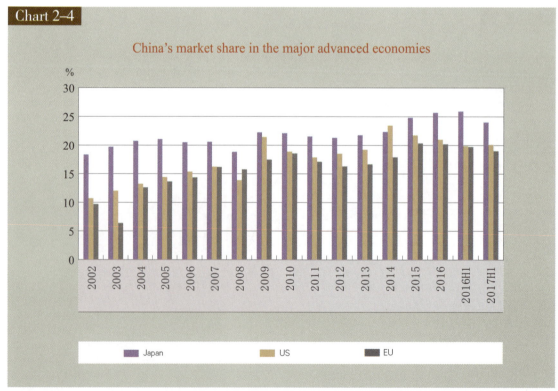

Chart 2–4

China's market share in the major advanced economies

Source: CEIC.

and 24 percent respectively, down by 0.7 percentage point and 2 percentage points year on year. In the meantime, China's exports and imports to Russia, Pakistan, Poland, and Kazakhstan increased by 33.1 percent, 14.5 percent, 24.6 percent, and 46.8 percent respectively.

(II) Trade in services

Trade in services grew rapidly. During the first half of 2017, China's trade in services totaled USD 337.8 billion, up by 9 percent year on year, whereas its trade in goods totaled USD 1839.5 billion, up by 15 percent year on year. The ratio of trade in services to trade in goods was 18 percent (see Chart 2–5). Insurance and pension services, financial services, and construction services decreased by 16 percent, 15 percent, and 8 percent respectively, while high value–added services, such as charges for the use of intellectual property, computer and information services, and traditional transport services, grew rapidly, up by 36 percent, 23 percent, and 15 percent respectively year on year.

Revenue from trade in services increased slightly. During the first half of 2017revenue from China's trade in services totaled USD 101.4 billion, a year–on–year increase of 0.4 percent (see Chart 2–6). Among the major items, travel revenue decreased by 12 percent, other commercial services decreased by 1 percent, and transport services increased by 8 percent. Among the

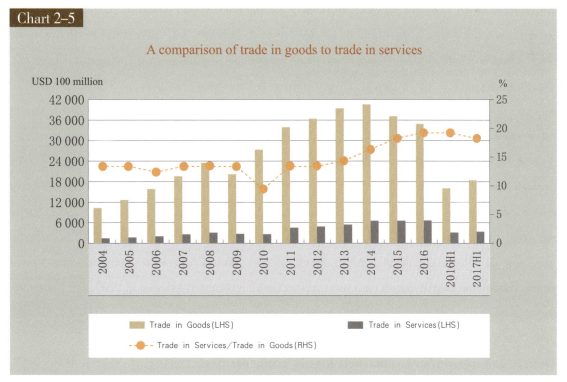

Chart 2–5

A comparison of trade in goods to trade in services

Trade in Goods(LHS)　　　Trade in Services(LHS)
Trade in Services/Trade in Goods(RHS)

Source: SAFE.

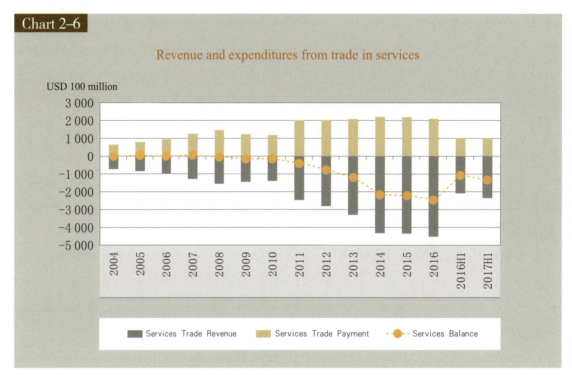

Chart 2–6

Revenue and expenditures from trade in services

Source: SAFE.

relatively small items, charges for the use of intellectual property increased by 4.5 times.

Expenditures for trade in services increased. During the first half of 2017expenditures for trade in services totaled USD 236.4 billion, a year–on–year increase of 13 percent. Among the major items, travel accounted for 57 percent of the total expenditures, a year–on–year increase of 13 percent. Transport accounted for 18 percent, a year–on–year increase of 18 percent. Other commercial services accounted for 9 percent, a year–on–year decrease of 5 percent. Charges for the use of intellectual property accounted for 6 percent, a year–on–year increase of 22 percent.

Trade in services remained in deficit. During the first half of 2017, trade in services recorded a deficit of USD 135.1 billion, a year–on–year increase of 24 percent. Travel remained the main source for the deficit (see Chart 2–7). During the first half of 2017, travel recorded a deficit of USD 115.9 billion, an increase of 19 percent year on year. With improved economic development and increased national income, more Chinese went abroad to travel and study. The second largest deficit item was transport, which recorded a deficit of USD 26.2 billion, an increase of 26 percent year on year. Due to the relatively large increase in China's imports of goods, cargo transport expenditures increased, contributing to a larger deficit in transport.

Deficit counter-parties remained highly concentrated. During the first half of 2017, China's top ten partners in terms of trade in services were Hong Kong SAR, the United States,

Chart 2–7

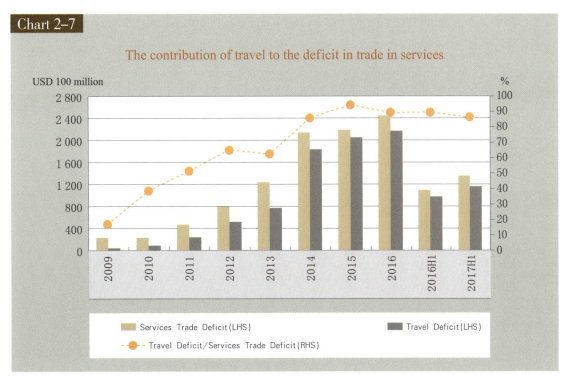

The contribution of travel to the deficit in trade in services

Source: SAFE.

Chart 2–8

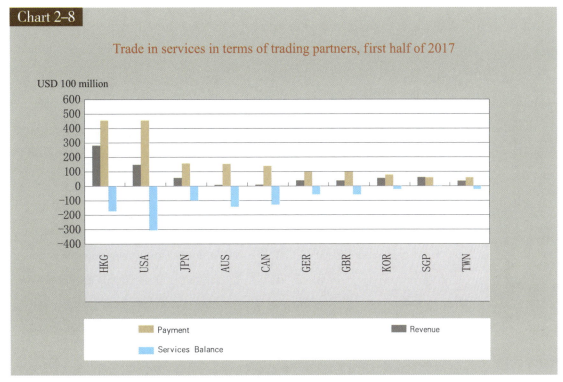

Trade in services in terms of trading partners, first half of 2017

Source: SAFE.

Japan, Australia, Canada, Germany, the United Kingdom, South Korea, Singapore, and China Taiwan.Trade in services with those economies amounted USD 246.4 billion, accounting for 73 percent of the total. With the exception of Singapore, China posted deficits with the other nine. The deficit with Hong Kong SAR, the United States, Australia, and Canada exceeded USD 10 billion respectively (see Chart 2–8). In particular, the United States ranked as China's largest deficit partner, followed by Hong Kong SAR, Australia, Canada and Japan.

Box 3

Innovations in foreign–exchange administration to support the development of cross–border e–commerce

Under the circumstances of international economic integrity and trade globalization, cross–border e–commerce brought about dramatic changes to the modes of international trade. For companies, cross–border e–commerce largely expanded their channels into international markets, optimized resource allocations, and brings mutual benefits and win–win results. For customers, cross–border e–commerce makes it easier to obtain goods and services abroad and to better meets personal needs.

In recent years, China's cross-border e-commerce has developed rapidly. According to statistics of the China e–commerce Research Center, China's cross–border e–commerce totaled RMB 6 trillion in 2016, an increase of 16.7 percent year on year. More than 5 000 platforms and 200 000 companies took part in cross–border e–commerce businesses. Compared with traditional trade, China's cross–border e–commerce transactions were small, dispersed, and convenient. First, buyers and sellers were directly matched online, which largely reduced intermediary processing and increased efficiency. Second, as the thresholds to participate declined, participants became more diversified, enabling more small companies and individuals to enter the market. Third, there have been progressive innovations in the settlement channels. For instance, settlements can be made either online by bank cards and third–party payments, or offline by bank cards. Fourth, the trade modes for cross–border e–commerce have been diversified, as follows:

Major trade modes for imports: For general merchandise, domestic e–commerce platforms declare imports in a traditional way after obtaining the orders. For individual cross–border parcel imports, domestic customers receive parcels from abroad after shopping online internationally. For bonded stocks, cross–border e–commerce platforms store the products in bonded warehouses in advance. The bonded warehouses deliver the ordered goods after declaring the imports directly to the customs.

The major trade modes for exports: In the comprehensive pilot zones, the Customs simplifies the export declarations, namely *verification according to the export list and reporting the aggregate* information. Goods are first delivered to overseas customers, and sellers declare aggregate parcel exports on a regular basis. For direct parcel exports, some e–commerce sellers directly deliver the products as parcels. For overseas warehouses, domestic e–commerce companies set up affiliated companies abroad and the products are exported in bulk as general merchandise to the overseas warehouses. Once the foreign clients place an order, the overseas warehouses are responsible for the delivery.

Foreign-exchange administration further facilitated foreign-exchange settlements for cross-border e-commerce. Currently, 13 cities, including Hangzhou and Tianjin, have established comprehensive national cross–border e–commerce pilot zones. Customs, inspections, tariffs, and foreign–exchange administration facilitate the cross–border e–commerce in those zones. For instance, the SAFE instituted a pilot for cross–border foreign–exchange payments for e–commerce through payment institutions. In 2015, the SAFE implemented this program throughout the country. The regional restrictions were lifted, the power of verification was delegated, the threshold for each single transaction was increased, and the scope of the payments was expanded. Meanwhile, the SAFE permitted individual businesses involved in cross–border e–commerce to open individual foreign–exchange settlement accounts to facilitate their cross–border receipts and payments. On a risk–controllable basis, the SAFE will continue to facilitate foreign–exchange settlements for cross–border e–commerce and will support the vigorous development of new foreign trade, such as cross–border e–commerce.

(III) Direct investments

Direct investments[①] **changed from net outflows to net inflows.** During the first half of 2017, China's direct investments on its balance–of–payments statement recorded a net inflow

---

① The net flow of direct investments refers to the gap between the net increase in direct–investment assets and the net increase in direct–investment liabilities. When the net increase in direct–investment assets is more than the net increase in direct–investment liabilities, a net outflow is recorded, and vice versa.

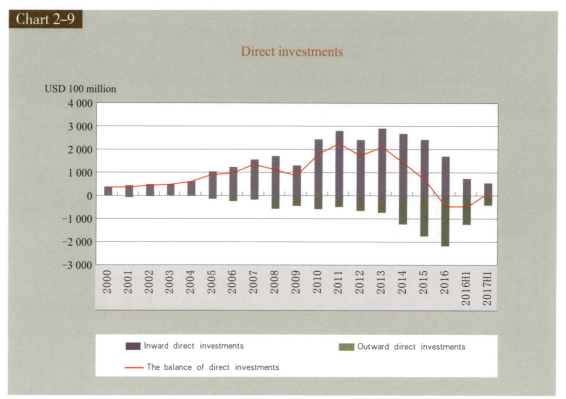

Source: SAFE.

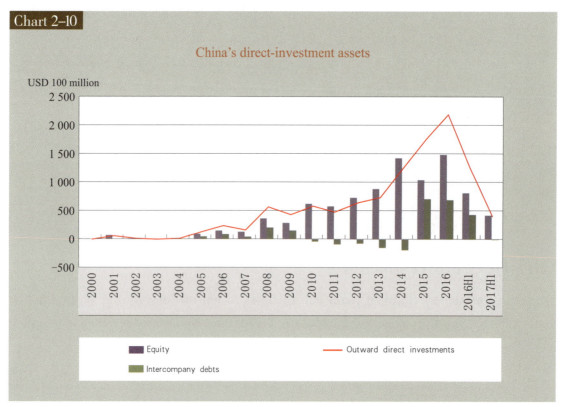

Source: SAFE.

of USD 13.9 billion (see Chart 2–9), whereas during the first half of 2016, this item recorded a net outflow of USD 49.4 billion. Direct investments changed from persistent outflows to inflows due to two reasons. First, Chinese enterprises became more rational so they slowed down their overseas investments. Second, inward foreign direct investments continued to flow into China.

Direct-investment assets[①] increased at a decreasing pace. During the first half of 2017, China's direct–investment assets (mainly China's outward direct investments) recorded a net increase of USD 41.1 billion, down by 67 percent year on year (see Chart 2–10).

In terms of the composition of the investments, equity–investment assets recorded a net increase of USD 41.9 billion, down by 48 percent year on year. Equity investments in direct investments are long–term investments. The slow down in the growth rate indicates that after years of rapid growth of outward direct investments, domestic enterprises became more rational about their outward investments in the context of the good performance of the domestic economy, the unstable international environment, and other uncertainties. Loan assets to overseas affiliates recorded a net increase of USD 68.8 billion, down by 2 percent year on year. In particular, this item recorded a net decrease of USD 0.8 billion, whereas during the first half of 2016, the item recorded a net increase of USD 43.1 billion. The change indicated that loans were becoming more flexible and vulnerable to short–term factors.

In term of sectors, direct–investment assets by the non–financial sector recorded a net increase of USD 31.8 billion, down by 71 percent year on year. The largest outward direct–investment destination was Hong Kong SAR, accounting for more than 60 percent of the total. Outward direct investments to the United States and the Cayman Islands together accounted for 22 percent of the total, indicating that China's outward direct–investment destinations were economies with relatively loose administrations, a pattern similar to that of global equity investments. In term of industries, manufacturing ranked the largest industry, accounting for 37 percent of the total and up by 14 percent, whereas during the first half of 2016, it ranked as the second largest. Leasing and business services accounted for 20 percent, down by 3 percent (see Chart 2–11). The direct–investment assets of the financial sector recorded a net increase of USD 9.3 billion, down by 41 percent. Banks and other financial institutions were the main contributors.

---

① A major component of direct–investment assets is outward direct investments. In addition, reverse investments by domestic foreign–funded enterprises to their parent companies are also included.

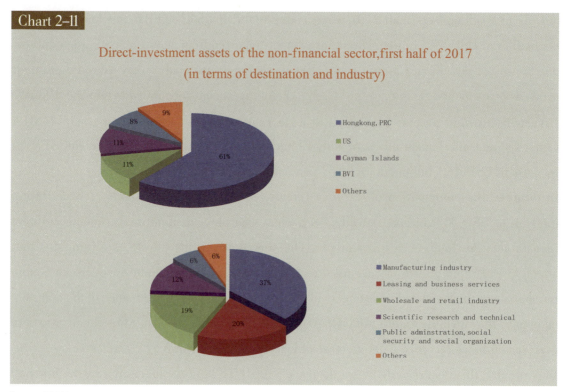

Source: SAFE.

Direct-investment liabilities^①maintained a significant net inflow. During the first half of 2017, direct–investment liabilities recorded a net increase of USD 55 billion, down by 26 percent year on year. In term of the composition of the investments, equity–investment liabilities recorded a net increase of USD 52 billion, down by 32 percent (see Chart 2–12). Equity investments remained stable, reflecting that China was continually attracting long–term foreign capital inflows as the investment environment improved. Loans from overseas affiliates posted a net increase of USD3 billion, whereas during the first half of 2016, investments decreased by USD 2 billion. This change shows that enterprises made financial arrangements according to the conditions in both the domestic and the international markets.

In term of sectors, direct–investment liabilities in the non–financial sector posted a net increase of USD 49.7 billion, down by 29 percent year on year and accounting for 90 percent of the total. As the Chinese economy progressively underwent transformation, foreign shareholders adjusted their investments accordingly. During the first half of 2017, leasing and business services once again were the most attractive for foreign direct investors, accounting

───────────

① Direct–investment liabilities are mainly composed of foreign direct investments. Reverse investments to domestic parent companies by overseas subsidiaries are also included.

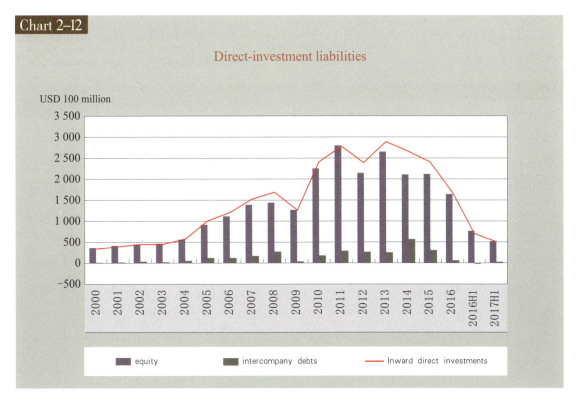

Chart 2–12

Direct-investment liabilities

USD 100 million

equity   intercompany debts   — Inward direct investments

Source: SAFE.

for 28 percent of the total and up by 19 percent. Wholesale and retailing ranked as second largest for FDI net inflows, accounting for 26 percent and up by 14 percent. Net flows into the real estate industry changed from a net increase to a net decrease. The main FDI source was still China Hong Kong SAR, followed by the Netherlands, China Taiwan province, and South Korea. The top four economies in terms off oreign direct investments remained the same as that in the first half of 2016. Direct–investment liabilities of the financial sector recorded a net inflow of USD 5.3 billion, up by 13 percent year on year. Foreign direct investments flowed mainly to banks in the form of reinvestments of earnings, indicating that the relatively good performance of domestic banks continued to attract foreign investments.

Box 4

During the first half of 2017, outward direct investments slowed down and their structure was optimized

After the expansion in 2015 and 2016 and impacted by the large base and the adjustment in the domestic and global economic conditions, during the first half of 2017 outward direct investments slowed down. However, the structure of outward direct investments was optimized and the quality improved. Outward direct investments by market entities tended to be stable and orderly. During the next stage the foreign—exchange administrative departments will continue to maintain the stability of the policies for outward direct investments and will make accommodations for new situations based on research.

Ⅰ The structure of outward direct investments was optimized during the first half of 2017

In terms of the growth rate, during the first half of 2017direct investments of non—financial enterprises in China to the real estate, culture, sports, and entertainment industries amounted to USD 1.5 billion, down by 82 percent from the previous year. If the data for these industries are deducted, outward direct investments totaled USD 46.7 billion, down by 23 percent from the previous year. As before, normal outward direct investments can carry out foreign—exchange registrations and purchases, and they can pay in foreign currency in accordance with the current regulations.

In terms of the proportion, during the first half of 2017 outward direct investments in the real estate, culture, sports, and entertainment industries accounted for 3 percent of the total outward investments by non—financial enterprises, 6 percent down from the first half of the previous year. Meanwhile, total capital flows to the leasing, manufacturing, wholesale and retail, information communications service, and software and information technology industries accounted for a higher percentage as compared to the same period of the previous year. The proportions were 28 percent, 18 percent, 13 percent, and 11percent respectively. Therefore, the structure and quality of outward direct investments generally further improved.

In terms of regions, during the first half of 2017 Chinese enterprises made new investments in the amount of USD 6.6 billion in the 47 One Belt and One Road countries, accounting for 14 percent of the total outward investments, up by 6 percent from the same period of the previous year.

Ⅱ The improvements in the structure of outward direct investments had a close relationship with the adjustments in of domestic and global economic conditions and the standardization of policies

First, as the domestic macroeconomy was stabilized and improved and the RMB exchange rate stabilized and followed an appreciating trend, market entities had a weaker demand for outward investments and for allocating assets overseas. On the one side, since 2017 our main economic indicators, such as GDP, the CPI, new urban employment, and the balance of payments, were all better than expected. Enterprises and individuals had stronger confidence in domestic economic development. On the other side, the RMB exchange rate against the USD faced obvious two-way fluctuations. The mid-price appreciated by 2.4 percent during the first half of 2017. Meanwhile, the formation mechanism for the RMB exchange rate against the USD was further optimized and counter-cyclical interventions began to show some effects. Under such conditions, domestic entities became more rational in terms of outward investments and preferred to remain in China.

Second, the measures to regulate outward direct investments began to have an effect. In order to promote the healthy development of outward direct investments while improving facilitation of outward investments, the National Development and Reform Commission, the Ministry of Commerce, the People's Bank of China, and the State Administration of Foreign Exchange strengthened the authenticity and compliance verifications for some irrational investments. The structure of outward investments was further optimized. Outward investments related to real estate, hotels, cinemas, entertainment, and sports clubs were largely reduced. Since 2017, the foreign-exchange administrative departments have continued to adjust and optimize the measures according to changes in the conditions. As of the present, the foreign-exchange policies for outward direct investments have returned to a normal situation and demand for foreign currency is stable and controllable.

In addition, Europe and United State shave strengthened their intervention in some acquisitions and mergers by national security reviews on foreign investments. To some extent, this had an impact onoutward investments by domestic entities.

For the next stage, the foreign-exchange administrative departments will cooperate with other departments responsible for the management of outward investments to continue support for qualified and capable domestic enterprises to carry out authentic and regulated outward direct investments and to actively support the productive capacity for One Belt and One Road construction and international cooperation. Meanwhile, on going facilitation and guarding against risks will both be emphasized. We will continue to guide domestic enterprises to invest in a rational way and to instruct financial institutions to strengthen their compliance and risk management for acquisition and merger loans and for domestic guarantees for overseas credit. We will crack down on illegal transactions, such as false and malicious guarantees. While promoting outward investments to develop in a healthy and orderly way, we will effectively maintain our foreign-related financial safety.

(IV) Portfolio investments

Net outflows of portfolio investments dropped. During the first half of 2017, portfolio investments recorded a net outflow of USD 19.5 billion, a year-on-year decline of 41 percent (see Chart 2-13), due to large gross inflows during the period. In terms of the composition of the investments, net outflows of equity investments and bond investments totaled USD 2.5 billion and USD 17 billion respectively, down by 80 percent and 16 percent year on year.

Outward portfolio investments grew slightly. During the first half of the year, China's outward portfolio investments increased by USD 40.1 billion (net outflows), representing year-on-year growth of 6 percent. In particular, equity investments and bond investments increased by USD14.2 billion and USD 25.9 billion respectively.

In terms of the major channels, first, domestic residents purchased foreign securities in the amount of USD 18 billion via the Shanghai - Hong Kong Connect and the Mutual Recognition

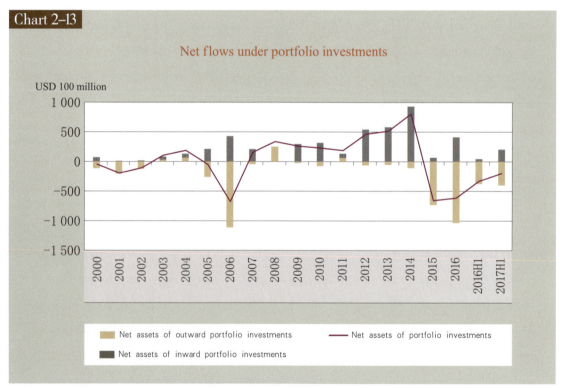

Chart 2-13

Net flows under portfolio investments

USD 100 million

Net assets of outward portfolio investments
Net assets of inward portfolio investments
Net assets of portfolio investments

Note: Positive outward portfolio investments indicate a decrease in outward investments in equities and bonds, and vice versa. Positive inward portfolio investments indicate an increase in inward investments in equities and bonds, and vice versa.
Source: SAFE.

of Funds. Second, net outward equity and bond investments by financial institutions recorded USD 15.5 billion. Third, net outflows by QDIIs and RQDIIs totaled USD 4.1 billion. Fourth, bonds issued by non–residents in the domestic market and purchased by residents totaled USD 2.5 billion.

Inward portfolio investments increased. During the first half of the year, inward portfolio investments recorded a net inflow of USD 20.6 billion, up by 350 percent year on year, indicating RMB assets were increasingly attractive for the allocation of global assets. In particular, inward equity investments recorded a net inflow of USD 11.6 billion, up by 87 percent. Inward bond investments recorded a net inflow of USD 9 billion, whereas during the first half of 2016 they had recorded a net outflow of USD 1.6 billion. In 2017, the further opening of the inter–bank bond market to foreign investors and the inclusion of the A–share stock market into the MSCI promoted capital inflows as well as market confidence.

In terms of the major channels, first, capital inflows via the Shanghai–Hong Kong Connect and the Shenzhen – Hong Kong Connect totaled USD 14.7 billion. Second, stocks and bonds issued by Chinese institutions in offshore markets and purchased by non–residents totaled USD 10.3 billion. Third, investments by foreign investors in the domestic bond market amounted to USD 8 billion. The main drivers for outflows included a decrease of USD 11.5 billion in inward investments by QFIIs and RQFIIs and a decline of USD 0.9 billion in outstanding bankers' acceptances with drafts.[1]

(V) Other investments

Other investments posted a net inflow. During the first half of 2017, an increase in net liabilities(net inflows) of USD 73.2 billion was registered for other investments, 88 percent higher than the net inflows of USD 39 billion for the financial account, whereas during the first half of 2016 other investments recorded an increase of USD 93.8 billion in net assets. In particular, net liabilities of currency and deposits increased by USD 91.3 billion, net assets of loans increased by USD 11.8 billion, and net liabilities of trade credits decreased by USD 4.3 billion.

Asset growth under other investments declined. During the first half of 2017,external assets under other investments grew by USD 53.6 billion, 29 percent less than the growth

---

[1] According to the Balance of Payment Manual (sixth edition), bankers' acceptances with drafts are moved from the category of other investments/loans to the category of portfolio investments/debt securities.

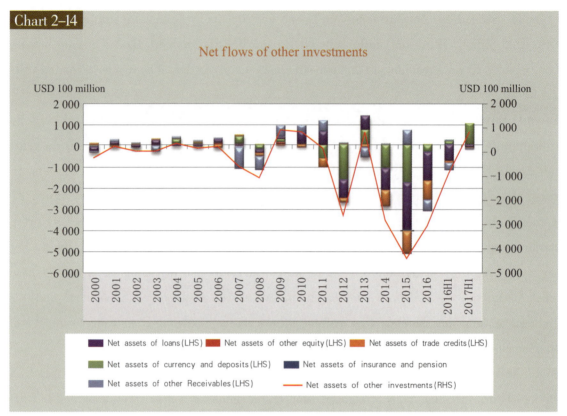

Chart 2–14

Net flows of other investments

USD 100 million   USD 100 million

Legend:
■ Net assets of loans (LHS)   ■ Net assets of other equity (LHS)   ■ Net assets of trade credits (LHS)
■ Net assets of currency and deposits (LHS)   ■ Net assets of insurance and pension
■ Net assets of other Receivables (LHS)   — Net assets of other investments (RHS)

Source: SAFE.

registered during the first half of 2016. Although domestic entities were still actively involved in international activities, overseas investments declined. This stable trend in overseas investments was attributed to the two–way fluctuations in the RMB exchange rate as well as to more rational market participants. During the first half of the year, in addition to direct investments and portfolio investments, growth of overseas loans and deposits and currencies was the main driver for outward investments, recording USD 66.5 billion and USD 8.3 billion respectively, while trade–credit assets (trade receivables and pre–paid) registered a decrease of USD 29.6 billion in the outstanding amount.

Liabilities of other investments changed from a decrease to an increase. During the first half of 2017, liabilities of other investments recorded an increase of USD 126.7 billion, whereas during the first half of 2016, they had recorded a decrease of USD 17.9 billion. The main changes included: first, the external debts borrowed by domestic enterprises rebounded and increased by USD 54.7 billion, whereas during the first half of 2016 they had decreased by USD 31.8 billion. The increased interest of domestic enterprises in borrowing external loans indicated the improvement in the Chinese economy and the enhanced market confidence.

Second, currency and deposits increased by USD 99.5 billion, 350 percent more than that during the first half of 2016. In particular, non–resident RMB deposits increased by USD 48.6 billion, whereas they had decreased by USD 8.1 billion during the first half of 2016. The dramatic growth in non–resident RMB deposits reflected the increased interest in RMB assets by foreign investors. Third, the decrease intrade–credit liabilities totaled USD 33.9 billion, 10 percent more than that during the first half of 2016.

Box 5

China deepened its economic connections with the belt–and–road countries

In 2013 China proposed the initiative to co–build the silk road economic belt and to co–construct a 21st century maritime silk road. Currently, more than 60 countries and international organizations have actively responded to this initiative. After four years of development and cooperation, China has deepened its economic connections with the belt–and–road countries, and it has recorded booming trade and investment with them. According to SAFE statistics on cross–border receipts and payments via domestic banks, [1] cross–border transactions between China and the belt–and–road countries totaled USD 1.1 trillion in 2016. During the first half of 2017, the volume totaled approximately USD 600 billion.

China and the belt-and-road countries experienced an expansion of trade and frequent economic connections. From 2013 to 2016, cross–border receipts and payments between China and the belt–and–road countries totaled USD 4.8 trillion, accounting for 19 percent of the total. Cross–border receipts amounted to USD 2.4 trillion, accounting for 20 percent of the total. Cross–border payments amounted to USD 2.3 trillion, accounting for 18 percent of the total. Singapore and South Korea were the top two countries that had large cross–border transactions with China. From 2013 to 2016, cross–border transactions between Chinese non–banks and Singapore amounted to USD 500 billion. Transactions between Chinese non–banks and South Korea amounted to USD 200 billion. Among the countries recording more than USD 10 billion in cross–border cash flows with China, Vietnam and Pakistan recorded the most rapid growth. From 2013 to 2016, annual cross–border

---

① Unlike the balance–of–payments and international–investment–position statistics, the SAFE's cross–border receipts–and–payments statistics mainly cover receipts and payments between domestic non–bank residents(both institutions and individuals) and non–resident institutions and individuals.

transactions between China and Vietnam and China and Pakistan increased by 1.5 times.

Trade in goods with the belt-and-road countries expanded. In 2016 China's cross-border receipts and payments of trade in goods totaled USD 3.9054 trillion. Those with the belt–and–road countries totaled USD 862.7 billion, accounting for 22 percent of the total and up by 2 percentage points compared with that in 2013. Due to the sluggish external demand, the declining prices of international commercial goods, and the rate hikes in the USD, China's trade in goods declined by 13 percent in 2016 as compared to that in 2013. As a result, trade in goods with the belt–and–road countries declined. However, the volume only declined by 6 percent, far less than the overall decline.

Trade in services with the belt-and-road countries increased, especially for the construction and travel services. In 2016 China's trade in services with the belt–and–road countries totaled USD 82.5 billion, up by 25 percent as compared with that in 2013. Travel, including study abroad and overseas tourism, was the largest item. Travel totaled USD 24.9 billion, up by 44 percent as compared with that in 2013. With the promotion of the belt–and–road initiative, Chinese deepened their understanding of the belt–and–road countries. Travel expenditures to those countries expanded rapidly. Among the service items, construction services grew most rapidly. In 2016 construction totaled USD 9.2 billion, up by 98 percent as compared with that in 2013. Under the belt–and–road initiative, China and the related countries can use their comparative advantages and complement one another. For instance, China deepened its cooperation in international production capacity and provided more infrastructure construction services.

Investments and financing became more active. In 2016 investments between China and the belt–and–road countries totaled USD 178.4 billion, up by 95 percent as compared with that in 2013. The growth rate was 4 percentage points more than that of overall investments. Investments and financing between China and the related countries were mainly enhanced by financial institutions such as the China Development Bank and the Asia Infrastructure Bank, and by means of buyer's credit and concessional loans. Consequently, large construction projects[1] and loans from China to the South Asian countries were on the rise.

In term of counter-parties, China has a relatively tight investment bond with Southeast Asia, with cross-border receipts and payments growing rapidly. In 2016

---

[1] According to the balance–of–payments statistical principles, long–term large–scale overseas construction projects belong to foreign direct investments.

the investments between China and 10 Southeast Asian countries totaled USD 127.4 billion, up by 1.4 times as compared with that in 2013. Investments between China and 18 Western Asian countries totaled USD 10.8 billion, up by 43 percent. Among the belt−and−road countries that had investments exceeding USD 1 billion, Kazakhstan, Singapore, and Pakistan were the top three countries in term of the growth rate. Cross−border investments between China and Kazakhstan, Singapore, and Pakistan increased by 2.2 times, 1.5 times, and 1.5 times respectively.

Domestically, eastern China is the main contributing region, whereas western China grew more rapidly due to its geographic advantages. In term of regions, the developed areas in China were the main contributing regions. In 2016cross−border receipts and payments of five major cities and provinces, including Beijing, Shanghai, Guangdong province, Jiangsu province, and Zhejiang province, with the belt−and−road countries amounted to USD 761.6 billion, more than 60 percent of the total. However, benefiting from their advantageous geographic locations, the 9 western Chinese provinces witnessed rapid growth in cross−border transactions with the belt−and−road countries. In 2016 these provinces recorded USD 66 billion in cross−border cash flows with the belt−and−road countries. In particular, compared with that in 2013, Guangxi province, Yunnan province, Gansu province, Qinghai province, and Ningxia province recorded two−digit growth rates, much higher than the national average growth rate of 4 percent.

With the rapid development in both the volume and growth rate of cross−border receipts and payments between China and the belt−and−road countries, the initiative has a great potential. As cooperation deepens in the field of trade, investments, technical exchanges, and so forth, the belt−and−road initiative may create the longest economic corridor in the world, larger markets, more employment, and wider future cooperation.

III.International Investment Position

China's external assets and liabilities [①] **were both on the rise.** At end–June 2017, China's external financial assets reached USD 6 644.6 billion, representing growth of 2.8 percent compared to end–December 2016 (similarly hereafter); external liabilities reached USD 4893.1 billion, up by 4.9 percent; and net assets reached USD 1 751.5 billion, down by 2.7 percent (see Chart 3–1).

Reserve assets remained the largest component of the total external assets, but the ratio of private-sector holdings continued to increase. Among the external financial assets, at end–June 2017 reserve assets amounted to USD 3 150.4 billion, up by 1.7 percent, of which USD 29 billion was due to BOP transactions and USD 23.5 billion was due to the change in exchange rates and prices other than BOP transactions. As the largest component, reserve

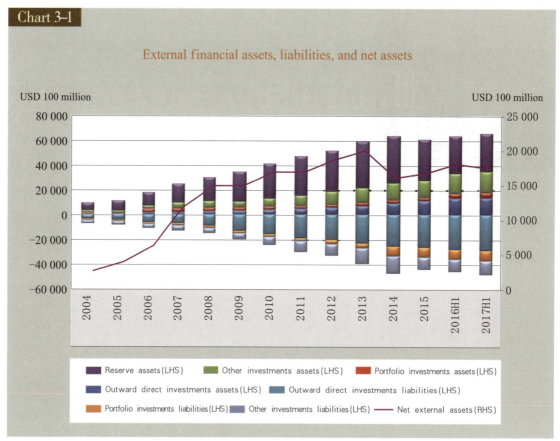

Chart 3–1

External financial assets, liabilities, and net assets

Source: SAFE.

---

① External financial assets and liabilities include direct investments, portfolio investments, and other investments, such as loans and deposits. Outward direct investments are included as financial assets because the equities issued by non–resident direct–investment enterprises and held by domestic investors are the same type of financial instruments as the equity investments in portfolio investments. The difference is that direct investments require a higher threshold of equity holdings so as to reflect a significant influence or control over the production and operations of the enterprises. Inward direct investments belong to external financial liabilities because foreign investors hold equities in foreign–owned companies.

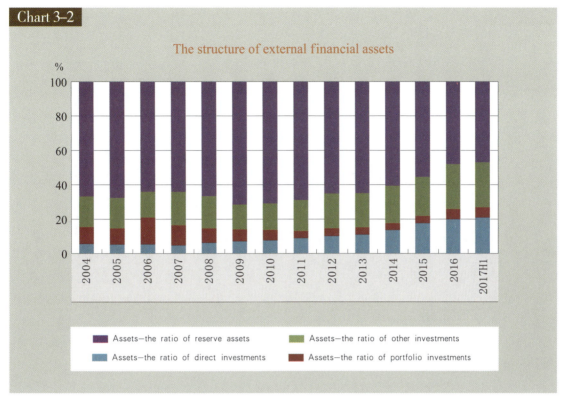

Chart 3–2

The structure of external financial assets

Legend:
Assets—the ratio of reserve assets
Assets—the ratio of direct investments
Assets—the ratio of other investments
Assets—the ratio of portfolio investments

Source: SAFE.

assets accounted for 47 percent of the total external assets, 1 percentage point less than that at end–December 2016 and a historical low since China's first IIP statement at end–December 2004. Direct–investment assets amounted to USD 1 369.7 billion, accounting for 21 percent of the total assets. Portfolio–investment assets amounted to USD 414.3 billion, accounting for 6 percent. Financial– derivative assets amounted to USD 6 billion, accounting for 0.1 percent. Other investments, such as loans and deposits, amounted to USD 1704.2 billion, accounting for 26 percent(see Chart 3–2).

Although foreign direct investments remained the major item in external liabilities, the proportion of other investment categories increased. Among the external liabilities, foreign direct investments (FDI) amounted to USD 2 924.5 billion at end–June 2017,[1] up by 2 percent. Continuing as the largest component, FDI accounted for 60 percent of the total external liabilities, 1 percentage point less than that at end–December 2016. Portfolio–investment liabilities amounted to USD 858.3 billion, accounting for 18 percent, 1 percentage

---

[1] The inward foreign direct investment position includes FDI stocks of both the non–financial sector and the financial sector. The position includes inter–company lending as well as other debt positions among the relevant offices. The statistics also reflect the impact of revaluations. The statistical coverage of inward FDI is different from the cumulative statistics of the Ministry of Commerce. Over the years, the latter used the cumulative FDI equity investment flows as the inward FDI position.

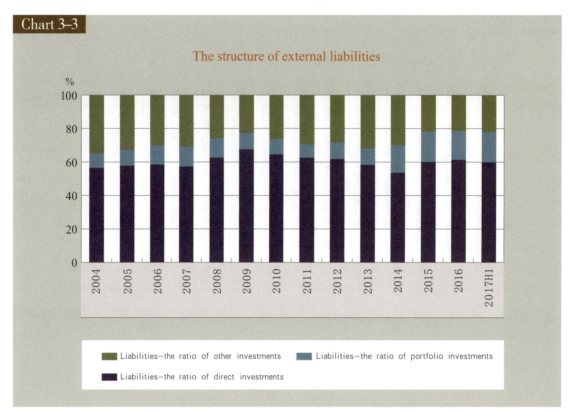

Source: SAFE.

point more than that at end–December 2016. Financial–derivative liabilities amounted to USD 4.9 billion, accounting for 0.1 percent. Other investments, such as loans and deposits, amounted to USD 1 105.4 billion, accounting for 23 percent, 1 percentage point more than that at end–December 2016 (see Chart 3–3).

Investment income remained indeficit. During the first half of 2017, China's investment income recorded a deficit of USD 12.2 billion, a year–on–year decline of 41 percent. Revenue from investments reached USD 113.0 billion, a year–on–year increase of 19 percent. Investment–income payments reached USD 125.2 billion, a year–on–year increase of 9 percent. The annualized yield difference between assets and liabilities was–2.4 percentage points, a narrowing by 0.2 percentage point compared with that in 2016 (see Chart 3–4). The structure of external financial assets and liabilities determined the deficit in the investment–income account. At end–June 2017, reserve assets accounted for almost half of the total assets, which were invested in assets with high liquidity. As a result, the average annualized yield of China's external assets from 2005 to the first half of 2017 was 3.3 percent. Among external liabilities, inward FDI was the major component. As long–term and stable investments, equity liabilities in inward FDI require a higher yield than other types of investments. From 2005

Chart 3-4

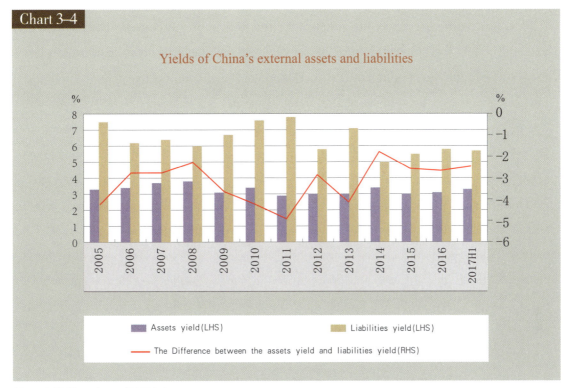

Yields of China's external assets and liabilities

Notes: 1. Yields on Assets (liabilities)

$$= \frac{\text{annualized revenues(payments) of investment income}}{(\text{positionsat the reference year-end} + \text{positionsat the previous year-end}) /2}$$

2.The difference between the yields of assets and liabilities =the yield of assets– the yield of liabilities.

Source: SAFE.

to the first half of 2017, the average annualized yield of external liabilities was 6.4 percent. Continuous inflows of FDI and high investment returns revealed that the long–term investment environment in China still had great attraction for foreign investors, and inward FDI also played a positive role in the development of the Chinese economy.

Box 6

An international comparison of the International Investment Position

The International Monetary Fund statistics revealed that at end–December 2016 China's external financial assets, liabilities, and net external assets were on the rise, as compared with those at end–December 2015, and China was the second largest creditor in the world. **In terms of external assets, China ranked eighth in the world, reaching USD 6.5** trillion and with reserve assets accounting for nearly 50 percent. The structure of external assets was more balanced in the major developed countries, and much less diversified in the developing countries. The proportion of portfolio investments (including financial derivatives, similarly hereafter) in total external assets for the developed countries was high, generally over 40 percent, and on average reserve assets accounted for less than 5 percent. Japan was an exception because its reserve assets accounted for 14 percent (see Chart C6–1). By contrast, in the developing countries reserve assets on average accounted for more than 30 percent. In particular, China's reserve assets reached USD 3.1 trillion, ranking first in the world and 2.5 times those of Japan, which ranked second (at USD 1.2 trillion).The proportion of portfolio–investment assets was relatively low in the developing countries, but in South Korea and South Africa it reached as high as 26 percent and 38 percent respectively. As for the proportion of direct–investment assets, a much smaller gap was noticed between the developed and the developing countries.

In terms of external liabilities, China ranked ninth in the world and reached USD 4.7 trillion, with inward FDI accounting for 60 percent. The developed countries absorbed international capital mainly via portfolio investments, while the developing

Chart C6–1

International comparison of the structure of external assets, end-December 2016

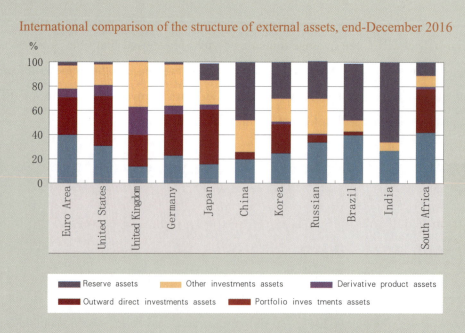

Sources: IMF, SAFE.

countries absorbed international capital mainly via FDI. The open financial markets in the developed countries determined that portfolio investments were the main channels for capital inflows. Portfolio–investment liabilities in the major developed countries, such as the United States, Japan, and the UK, accounted for more than 50 percent of the total liabilities (see Chart C6–2). In contrast, the developing countries mainly relied on FDI. FDI liabilities in the developing countries, such as China, Brazil, and Russia, accounted for 61 percent, 53percent, and 46percent of the total liabilities respectively. As exceptions, South Korea and South Africa had a low proportion of FDI, and portfolio investments accounted for 63 percent and 53 percent respectively. The proportion of other investments, such as loans and deposits, were dispersed among the major countries, ranging from 13 percent to 41 percent.

Chart C6–2

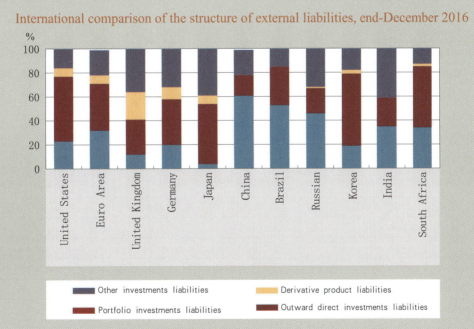

International comparison of the structure of external liabilities, end-December 2016

Sources: IMF, SAFE.

In terms of net external assets, Japan had the largest net external assets, whereas the United States had the largest net external liabilities. China ranked as the second largest creditor, with USD 1.8 trillion in net external assets. At end–December 2016, Japan ranked first, with USD 3.0 trillion in net external assets, followed by China (USD 1.8 trillion) as second, and Germany (USD 1.8 trillion) as third(see Chart C6–1). The United States was the largest debtor in the world, with USD 8.1 trillion in net external liabilities at end–December 2016, followed by Spain and Australia with USD 1.0 trillion and USD 0.7 trillion respectively. The UK had both large external assets and large external liabilities of equivalent scales, so its net external assets totaled only USD 0.6 trillion.

Table C6-1 International comparison of external assets and liabilities, end-December 2016 Unit：100 million USD

Countries/Regions	Net assets	Assets	Liabilities
Japan	29 889	85 424	55 535
China	18 005	64 666	46 660
Germany	17 973	87 092	69 119
Hong Kong,PRC	11 807	45 779	33 973
Switzerland	8 393	44 036	35 642
Norway	7 341	15 332	7 991
The United Kingdom	5 757	136 553	130 796
Mexico	-4 822	5 824	10 646
Ireland	-5 193	51 516	56 709
Brazil	-7 166	7 733	14 899
Australia	-7 389	16 111	23 500
Spain	-10 057	18 688	28 745
USA	-81 096	239 167	320 263

Sources: IMF, SAFE.

Table 3-1 China's International Investment Position, end-June 2017

Unit: 100 million USD

Items	Line No.	2017H1
Net International Investment Position	1	17 515
Assets	2	66 446
1 Direct investment	3	13 697
1.1 Equity and investment fund shares	4	11 178
1.2 Debt instruments	5	2 519
1.a Financial sector	6	2 213
1.1.a Equity and investment fund shares	7	2 119
1.2.a Debt instruments	8	94
1.b Non-financial sector	9	11 484
1.1.b Equity and investment fund shares	10	9 059
1.2.b Debt instruments	11	2 425
2 Portfolio investment	12	4 143
2.1 Equity and investment fund shares	13	2 546
2.2 Debt securities	14	1 597

(Continued)

Items	Line No.	2017H1
3 Financial derivatives (other than reserves) and employee stock options	15	60
4 Other investment	16	17 042
4.1 Other equity	17	55
4.2 Currency and deposits	18	3 816
4.3 Loans	19	6 373
4.4 Insurance, pension, and standardized guarantee schemes	20	105
4.5 Trade credit and advances	21	5 849
4.6 Other accounts receivable	22	844
5 Reserve assets	23	31 504
5.1 Monetary gold	24	736
5.2 Special drawing rights	25	100
5.3 Reserve position in the IMF	26	95
5.4 Foreign currency reserves	27	30 568
5.5 Other reserve assets	28	5
Liabilities	29	48 931
1 Direct investment	30	29 245
1.1 Equity and investment fund shares	31	27 078
1.2 Debt instruments	32	2 167
1.a Financial sector	33	1 391
1.1.a Equity and investment fund shares	34	1 299
1.2.a Debt instruments	35	92
1.b Non-financial sector	36	27 854
1.1.b Equity and investment fund shares	37	25 779
1.2.b Debt instruments	38	2 075
2 Portfolio investment	39	8 583
2.1 Equity and investment fund shares	40	6 221
2.2 Debt securities	41	2 362
3 Financial derivatives (other than reserves) and employee stock options	42	49
4 Other investment	43	11 054
4.1 Other equity	44	0
4.2 Currency and deposits	45	4 177
4.3 Loans	46	3 910
4.4 Insurance, pension, and standardized guarantee schemes	47	95
4.5 Trade credit and advances	48	2 544
4.6 Other accounts payable	49	232
4.7 Special drawing rights	50	97

Source: SAFE.

IV. Operation of the Foreign-Exchange
Market and the RMB Exchange Rate

(I) Trends in the RMB Exchange Rate

The RMB exchange rate against the USD showed an appreciation. At the end of June 2017, the mid–price of the RMB exchange rate against the USD was 6.7744, an appreciation of 2.4 percent from the end of 2016.The RMB spot exchange rate against the USD in the inter–bank foreign–exchange market (CNY) and in the offshore market (CNH) appreciated by 2.4 percent and 2.9 percent respectively (see Chart 4–1). The daily average spread between the CNH and the CNY was 189 bps (see Chart 4–2), higher than the 134 bps in 2016.

At the end of June 2017, the mid–price of the RMB exchange rate against the EUR,100JPY, GBP,AUD and CAD stood at7.7496,6.0485,8.8144,5.2099, and 5.2144respectively, a depreciation of 5.7 percent, 1.5 percent, 3.5 percent,3.7percent,and 1.4 percent respectively.

The RMB exchange rate depreciated slightly against the basket of currencies. According to CFETS data, at the end of June 2017 the RMB exchange–rate indexes of the CFETS, the BIS basket of currencies, and the SDR basket of currencies were 93.29, 94.25, and 94.18respectively, a depreciation of 1.6 percent, 2.1 percent, and 1.4 percent respectively from the end of the previous year.

According to the BIS, the nominal effective exchange rate of the RMB depreciated by 2.3 percent in the first half of 2017. Deducting for inflation, the real effective exchange rate of the

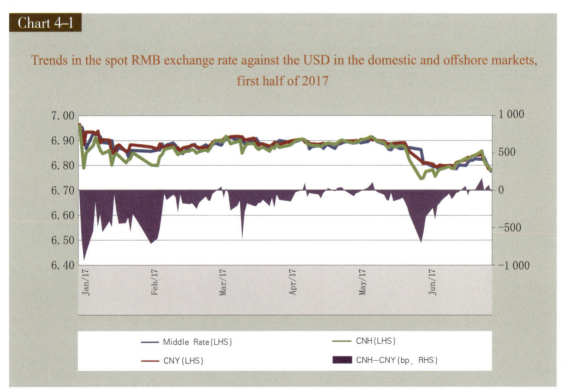

Chart 4–1

Trends in the spot RMB exchange rate against the USD in the domestic and offshore markets, first half of 2017

— Middle Rate(LHS) — CNH(LHS)
— CNY(LHS) ■ CNH–CNY(bp, RHS)

Sources: CFETS, Reuters.

Operation of the Foreign-Exchange Market and the RMB Exchange Rate | China's Balance of Payments Report
First Half of 2017

113

Chart 4-2

Spread of spot RMB exchange rates against the USD in the domestic and offshore markets

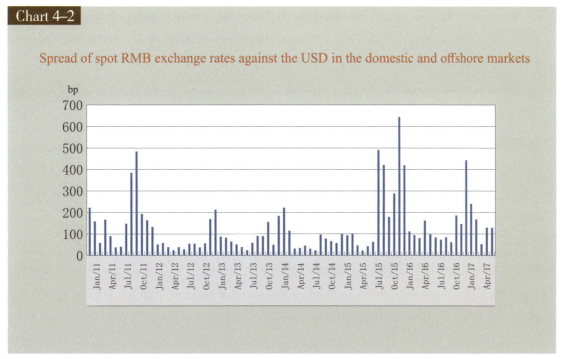

Note: The absolute values of the average daily spread.
Sources: CFETS, Reuters.

Chart 4-3

Trends in the effective RMB exchange rate

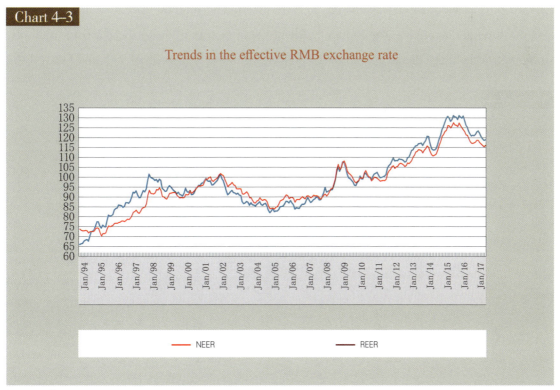

Source: BIS.

RMB depreciated by 3.3 percent (see Chart 4–3). Since the reform of the exchange–rate regime in 2005, the nominal and real effective exchange rates of the RMB appreciated by34.3 percent and 42.3 percent respectively. Among the 61 currencies observed by the BIS, the RMB ranked third and second respectively. From a medium– and long–term perspective, the RMB is still the most stable currency in the world.

Expectations regarding the RMB exchange rate were stable. During the first half of 2017, the domestic economy stabilized and had a better orientation. The USD continued to weaken. A counter–cyclical factor was introduced to the mid–price quoting model. The domestic and overseas market environments and the foreign–exchange rate formation mechanism each offered support for a basically stable RMB exchange rate. At the end of June, the one–year historical volatility of the RMB exchange rate in the domestic and offshore markets stood at 2.6 percent and 3.4 percent, down by 6.8 percent and 1.8 percent from the beginning of 2017 respectively. The implied volatilities in the domestic and offshore options markets reached 3.4 percent and 4.7 percent, down by 34.8 percent and 41.6 percent from the beginning of 2017 respectively (see Chart 4–4). The depreciation expectation for the RMB was largely weakened.

The RMB weakened in the foreign-exchange forward market. During the first half of 2017, the irrational and panic demands for purchasing foreign exchange were mitigated. Net forward purchases of foreign exchange were reduced. The interest–rate spread of the RMB and the foreign currencies was reduced. All of these factors allowed the RMB to gradually strengthen in both the domestic and overseas forward markets (see Chart 4–5 and Chart 4–6).

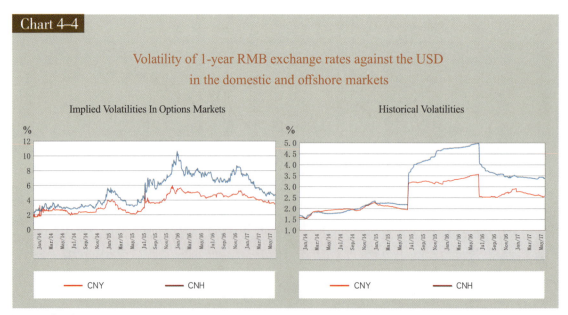

Chart 4–4

Volatility of 1-year RMB exchange rates against the USD in the domestic and offshore markets

Source: Bloomberg.

Operation of the Foreign-Exchange Market and the RMB Exchange Rate | China's Balance of Payments Report
First Half of 2017

115

Chart 4-5

The 1-year RMB exchange rate against the USD in the domestic and offshore markets

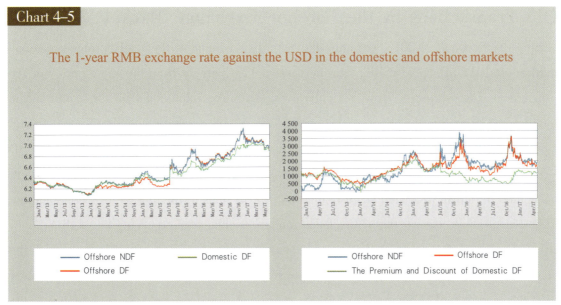

Sources: CFETS, Reuters.

During the first half of 2017, the one-year RMB/USD domestic delivered forward rate, the offshore delivered forward rate, and the offshore delivered forward rate without the principal rose by 1.7 percent, 5.3 percent, and 5.6 percent respectively.

Chart 4-6

The 6-month interest-rate spread of the domestic RMB and the USD

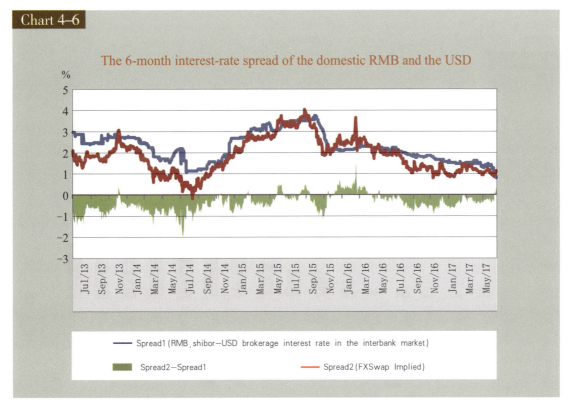

Sources: CFETS, Reuters.

(II) Transactions in the Foreign-Exchange Market

During the first half of 2017, the cumulative trading volume of the RMB/foreign-currency market totaled USD 10.49 trillion, an increase of 17.8 percent from the same period of the previous year (see Chart 4-7), with a daily average trading volume of USD 88.1 billion. The total trading volume in the client market and the inter-bank market was USD 1.79 trillion and USD 8.69 trillion respectively. Spot and derivative transactions saw a trading volume of USD 4.39 trillion and USD 6.09 trillion respectively (see Table 4-1). Derivatives, at 58.1 percent, accounted for a historical high share of the total transactions in the foreign-exchange market. This structure was closer to that of the global foreign-exchange market (see Chart 4-8).

Steady growth of foreign-exchange spot transactions. During the first half of 2017, the spot foreign-exchange market saw a trading volume of USD 4.39 trillion, up by 10.1 percent from the same period of the previous year. Spot purchases and sales of foreign exchange in the client market totaled USD 1.49 trillion (including banks, but excluding the implementation of forwards), up by 2.3 percent from the same period of the previous year. The spot inter-bank foreign-exchange market saw a trading volume of USD 2.9 trillion, up by 14.6 percent from the same period of the previous year. The share of USD transactions was 96.3 percent.

A recovery in foreign-exchange forward transactions. During the first half of 2017, the

Chart 4-7

Trading volume in China's foreign-exchange market

USD 100 million

Sources: SAFE, CFETS.

Operation of the Foreign-Exchange Market and the RMB Exchange Rate | China's Balance of Payments Report
First Half of 2017

117

Chart 4-8

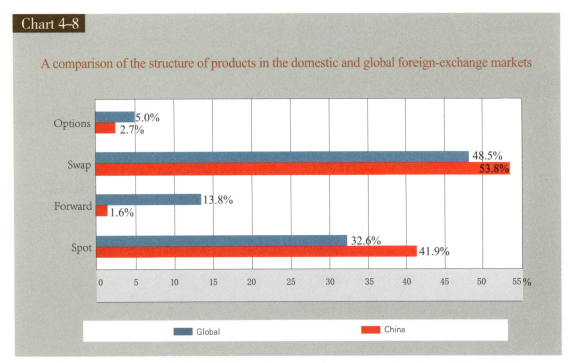

A comparison of the structure of products in the domestic and global foreign-exchange markets

Note: The data for China are from the first half of 2017; the global data are from a survey conducted by the BIS in April 2016.
Sources: SAFE, CFETS, BIS.

forward market saw a trading volume of USD 169.5 billion, up by 11.1 percent from the same period of the previous year. In the client market, purchases and sales of forwards in foreign exchange totaled USD 129 billion, up by 19.1 percent from the same period of the previous year. Purchases and sales of forwards were USD 69.3 billion and USD 59.8 billion, up by 94.3 percent and down by 17.8 percent respectively. Short-term 6-month transactions accounted for 67.1 percent of the total transactions, up by 7.8 percent from the same period of the previous year. In the inter-bank foreign-exchange market, forwards totaled USD40.4 billion, down by 8.5 percent from the same period of the previous year.

Swap transactions continued to rise. During the first half of 2017, cumulative foreign-exchange and currency-swap transactions totaled USD 5.6 trillion, up by 25.6 percent from the same period of the previous year. Cumulative foreign-exchange and currency-swap transactions in the client market reached USD 50.6 billion, down by 6.5 percent from the same period of the previous year. Spot purchases/forward sales and spot sales/forward purchases stood at USD 38.1 billion and USD 12.5 billion respectively, up by 27.9 percent and down by 48.7 percent from the same period of the previous year respectively. This mainly reflected the impact of the forward-rate adjustment on foreign-exchange liquidity and the financing management of market entities. The cumulative foreign-exchange and currency-swap transactions in the inter-bank

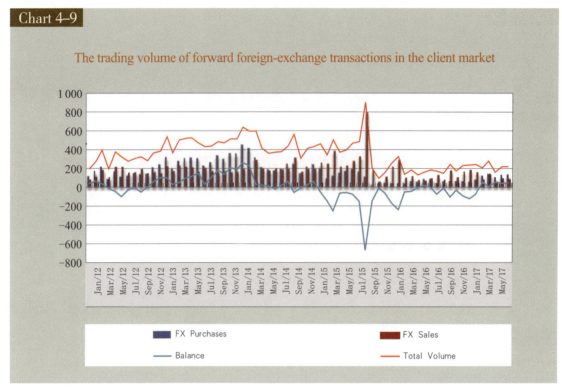

Chart 4–9

The trading volume of forward foreign-exchange transactions in the client market

FX Purchases   FX Sales

Balance   Total Volume

Source: SAFE.

market reached USD 5.6 trillion, up by 26 percent from the same period of the previous year.

A slight increase in option transactions. During the first half of 2017, the trading volume of options totaled USD 280.7 billion, up by 4.8 percent from the same period of the previous year. The client market saw a total trading volume of USD 121.4 billion, up by 44.2 percent from the same period of the previous year. The two–directional fluctuations in the RMB exchange rate shows that options have flexibility and an attraction when managing exchange–rate risks. The inter–bank market saw a total trading volume of USD 159.3 billion, down by 13.3 percent from the same period of the previous year.

Foreign-exchange market participants remained stable. Proprietary transactions by banks continued to dominate (see Chart4–10). The share of inter–bank transactions among all foreign–exchange transactions was 82.3 percent during the first half of 2017.The share of bank transactions with non–financial customers and non–banking financial institutions was 16.9 percent and 0.9 percent, basically the same as that in 2016.

Operation of the Foreign–Exchange Market and the RMB Exchange Rate | China's Balance of Payments Report
First Half of 2017

119

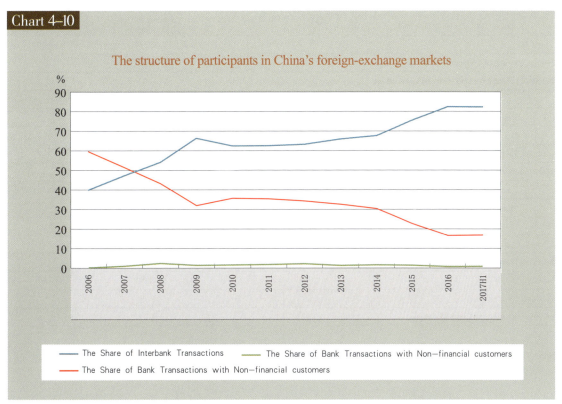

Chart 4–10

The structure of participants in China's foreign-exchange markets

— The Share of Interbank Transactions — The Share of Bank Transactions with Non–financial customers

— The Share of Bank Transactions with Non–financial customers

Sources: SAFE, CFETS.

Table 4-1   Transactions in the RMB/foreign-exchange market, first half of 2017

Products	Trading Volume (100 million USD)
Spot	43 949
Client Market	14 924
Interbank Foreign Exchange Market	29 025
Forward	1 695
Client Market	1 290
Less than 3 months (including 3 months)	636
3 months to 1 year (including 1 year)	568
More than 1 year	87
Interbank Foreign Exchange Market	404
Less than 3 months (including 3 months)	266
3 months to 1 year (including 1 year)	123
More than 1 year	15
Foreign Exchange and Currency Swaps	56 412
Client Market	506
Interbank Foreign Exchange Market	55 906
Less than 3 months (including 3 months)	48 402
3 months to 1 year (including 1 year)	7 451
More than 1 year	53
Options	2 807

(Continued)

Products	Trading Volume (100 million USD)
Client Market	1 214
Foreign Exchange Call Options/RMB Put Options	607
Foreign Exchange Put Options/RMB Call Options	607
Less than 3 months (including 3 months)	281
3 months to 1 year (including 1 year)	758
More than 1 year	175
Interbank Foreign Exchange Market	1 593
Less than 3 months (including 3 months)	1 075
3 months to 1 year (including 1 year)	513
More than 1 year	5
Total	104 863
Client Market	17 935
Interbank Foreign Exchange Market	86 928
Including: Spots	43 949
Forwards	1 695
Foreign Exchange and Currency Swaps	56 412
Options	2 807

Note: The trading volumes here are all unilateral transactions and the data employ rounded-off numbers.
Sources: SAFE, CFETS.

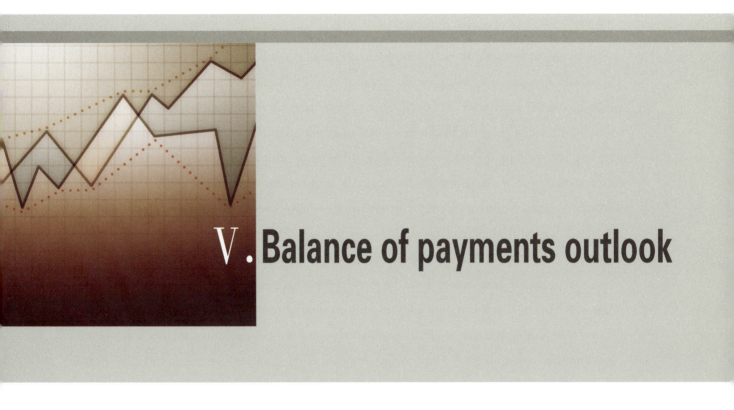

V. Balance of payments outlook

In the second half of 2017 China's balance of payments is expected to maintain a basic equilibrium.

The current account will maintain a reasonable surplus. First, the surplus in the trade in goods account will expand. In term of exports, the global economy will generally continueits recovery with astabilized momentum, contributing to stable external demand for Chinese goods. According to the IMF's July 2017 forecast, the global economy will grow at 3.5 percent and 3.6 percent in 2017 and 2018 respectively, higher than that in the previous two years. The advanced economies will grow by2.0 percent in 2017 and 1.9 percent in 2018, and the emerging market economies will grow by 4.6 percent and 4.8 percent during the same periods. In addition, stable progress in the belt-and-road initiative and cooperation in international capacity will benefit regional commerce. Further more, the major holidays in the Western countries will also promote seasonal exports. In terms of imports, as the performance of the domestic economy remains steady and continues to improve, and international commodity prices will hopefully stabilize after the previous rebound, China's imports will continue to grow steadily. Second, the deficit in trade in services will maintain basically stable growth. As a major deficit item in trade in services, the travel deficit has gradually reached a stable scale, as demand for overseas tourism and study has been released relatively quickly over the past two years. Third, during the past several years the structure of China's foreign financial assets has been continuously optimized. Outward investments other than reserve assets have increased progressively and have begun to produce more earnings. As a result, overall income from overseas investments will grow and the deficits in investment income will narrow. On the whole, the ratio of the surplus in the current account to GDP will remain within a reasonable range in 2017.

Cross-border capital flows will continue their overall stability. Conditions for the overall stability of cross-border capital flows in China will continue to exist in the future.First, the domestic economy is more stable and sustainable, and marked by good momentum. In 2017 the IMF repeatedly revised upward its forecast for China's economic growth.Representing an objective internation aljudgment, the recent forecast expected growth of the Chinese economy at 6.7 percent in 2017, the same as the growth in 2016. Second, the domestic market is more open. For example, a recent series of major measures in favor of foreign investment has been introduced, and FDI will remain basically stable as the relevant measures are progressively implemented. As the Bond Connect has been officially launched and the A-share stock market will be included in the MSCI emerging market index, foreign investors will be positively influenced to invest in the domestic securities market. In addition, the macro-prudential management policy of full–caliber cross–border financing will continue to prevent risks as well as to facilitate enterprise financing. Third, market expectations and the external balance–sheet adjustments of domestic enterprises will befurther stabilized. At present, as the RMB exchange–rate formation mechanismis continuously improving, domestic investors are becoming more rational about overseas investments, and as the foreign debt is recovering steadily, these factors will contribute to an improvement in the overall economic situation, additionally driving improvements in market expectations and promoting a virtuous cycle of equilibrium in the balance of payments. Moreover, as the current normalization process of the Fed monetary policy is basically in line with market expectations, its impact on the market, especially on boosting the dollar, will be weakened. If the exchange rate of the USD remainsstable, this will help to stabilize China's cross–border capital flows. Uncertainties, however, remain in the macroeconomic environment, including the economic development in the United States and Europe, the contagious effects on international foreign–exchange markets due to their monetary–policy adjustments, the impacts on international trade from trade protectionism, and so forth. It is necessary to dynamically evaluate the impact from those uncertainties on China's international balance of payments and cross–border capital flows. In addition, in the long run China's surplus in the current account will gradually be narrowed to within a reasonable range, andinward and outward FDI will present a reciprocal development trend. Therefore, the influence of these changes on the structure and the equilibrium in China's balance of payments will also require continuous attention.

During the second half of 2017, the SAFE will continue to study and implement the gist of the National Financial Work Conference in accordance with the unified deployment of the CPC Central Committee and the State Council, and it will focus on the three tasks of serving the real economy, guarding against financial risks, and deepening financial reform. Specifically, on the one hand, the SAFE will adhere to the reform and opening up, improve the foreign–exchange policy framework, support and promote the two–way opening of financial markets, promote capital account convertibility in an orderly and prudential manner, enhance the level of cross–border trade and investment facilitation, and serve the real economy; on the other hand, the SAFE will guard against risks from cross–border capital flows, build a prudential macro management system for cross–border capital flows, and a micro market regulatory system, maintain foreign–exchange market stability, and create a healthy, optimum and stable market environment for the reform and opening.

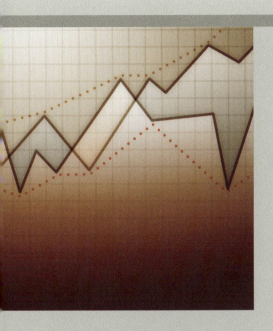

2017 上半年
First Half of 2017

中 国 国 际 收 支 报 告
China's Balance of Payments Report

附　　录　统计资料
Appendix　Statistics

一、国际收支 ①

I. Balance of Payments

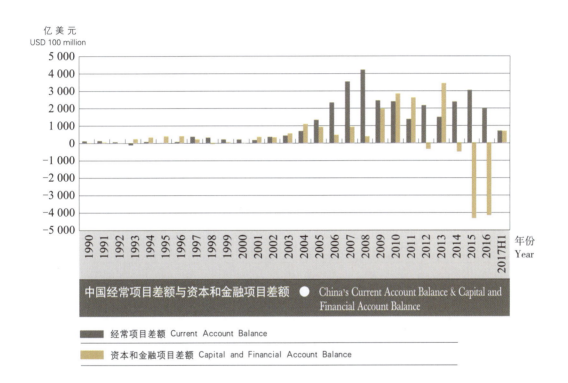

亿 美 元
USD 100 million

中国经常项目差额与资本和金融项目差额 ● China's Current Account Balance & Capital and Financial Account Balance

经常项目差额 Current Account Balance
资本和金融项目差额 Capital and Financial Account Balance

---

① 资料来源：国家外汇管理局；IMF《国际收支统计》、《国际金融统计》；环亚经济数据库。

Sources: State Administration of Foreign Exchange; IMF, Balance of Payments Statistics, International Financial Statistics; CEIC Database.

中国国际收支概览表（1）

China's Balance of Payments Abridged(1)

项目 / 年份 Item / Year	1982	1983	1984	1985	1986	1987
1.经常账户Current account	57	42	20	−114	−70	3
贷方Credit	243	240	273	276	276	354
借方Debit	−186	−198	−253	−390	−347	−351
A.货物和服务Goods and services	48	26	1	−125	−74	3
贷方Credit	226	220	248	258	262	341
借方Debit	−178	−194	−247	−383	−336	−338
a.货物Goods	42	18	−2	−131	−90	−13
贷方Credit	199	192	217	227	223	300
借方Debit	−158	−174	−219	−358	−313	−313
b.服务Services	6	8	2	6	16	16
贷方Credit	27	28	31	31	39	41
借方Debit	−20	−20	−29	−25	−23	−25
B.初次收入Primary income	4	12	15	8	0	−2
贷方Credit	10	15	19	14	9	10
借方Debit	−6	−3	−4	−5	−9	−12
C.二次收入Secondary income	5	5	4	2	4	2
贷方Credit	7	6	6	4	5	4
借方Debit	−2	−1	−2	−2	−1	−2
2.资本和金融账户 Capital and financial account	−60	−41	−32	139	83	11
2.1 资本账户Capital account	0	0	0	0	0	0
贷方Credit	0	0	0	0	0	0
借方Debit	0	0	0	0	0	0
2.2 金融账户Financial account	−60	−41	−32	139	83	11

单位：亿美元
Unit: USD 100 million

项目 / 年份 Item / Year	1982	1983	1984	1985	1986	1987
资产Credit	−71	−54	−58	50	13	−58
负债Debit	11	13	25	89	70	69
2.2.1 非储备性质的金融账户 Financial account excluding reserve assets	−17	−14	−38	85	65	27
资产Credit	−29	−27	−63	−4	−4	−42
负债Debit	11	13	25	89	70	69
直接投资Direct investment	4	8	13	13	18	17
资产Credit	0	−1	−1	−6	−5	−6
负债Debit	4	9	14	20	22	23
证券投资Portfolio investment	0	−6	−16	30	16	11
资产Credit	0	−6	−17	23	0	−1
负债Debit	0	0	1	8	16	12
金融衍生工具 Financial derivatives (other than reserves) and employee stock options	0	0	0	0	0	0
资产Credit	0	0	0	0	0	0
负债Debit	0	0	0	0	0	0
其他投资Other investment	−21	−16	−34	41	32	0
资产Assets	−28	−19	−44	−20	1	−34
负债Liabilities	6	4	10	62	31	34
2.2.2 储备资产Reserve assets	−42	−27	5	54	17	−17
其中:外汇储备 Foreign exchange reserves	−43	−19	7	56	12	−15
3.净误差与遗漏 Net errors and omissions	3	−2	12	−25	−12	−14

中国国际收支概览表（2）

China's Balance of Payments Abridged(2)

项目 / 年份 Item / Year	1994	1995	1996	1997	1998	1999
1.经常账户 Current account	77	16	72	370	315	211
贷方Credit	1 121	1 389	1 645	1 986	1 990	2 124
借方Debit	−1 045	−1 373	−1 573	−1 617	−1 675	−1 913
A.货物和服务 Goods and services	74	120	176	428	438	306
贷方Credit	1 046	1 319	1 548	1 874	1 888	1 987
借方Debit	−973	−1 199	−1 373	−1 446	−1 449	−1 681
a.货物Goods	35	128	122	366	456	329
贷方Credit	844	1 074	1 268	1 532	1 637	1 693
借方Debit	−810	−947	−1 147	−1 167	−1 181	−1 364
b.服务Services	39	−8	54	63	−18	−23
贷方Credit	202	244	280	342	251	294
借方Debit	−163	−252	−226	−280	−268	−317
B.初次收入 Primary income	−10	−118	−124	−110	−166	−145
贷方Credit	57	52	73	57	56	83
借方Debit	−68	−170	−198	−167	−222	−228
C.二次收入 Secondary income	13	14	21	51	43	49
贷方Credit	18	18	24	55	47	54
借方Debit	−4	−4	−2	−3	−4	−4
2.资本和金融账户 Capital and financial account	21	162	83	−147	−127	−33
2.1 资本账户 Capital account	0	0	0	0	0	0
贷方Credit	0	0	0	0	0	0
借方Debit	0	0	0	0	0	0
2.2 金融账户 Financial account	21	162	83	−147	−127	−33

单位：亿美元
Unit: USD 100 million

项目 / 年份 Item / Year	1994	1995	1996	1997	1998	1999
资产Credit	−367	−247	−357	−788	−479	−452
负债Debit	389	409	440	641	352	419
2.2.1 非储备性质的 金融账户 **Financial account excluding reserve assets**	326	387	400	210	−63	52
资产Credit	−62	−22	−40	−431	−415	−367
负债Debit	389	409	440	641	352	419
直接投资 **Direct investment**	318	338	381	417	411	370
资产Credit	−20	−20	−21	−26	−26	−18
负债Debit	338	358	402	442	438	388
证券投资 **Portfolio investment**	35	8	17	69	−37	−112
资产Credit	−4	1	−6	−9	−38	−105
负债Debit	39	7	24	78	1	−7
金融衍生工具 **Financial derivatives (other than reserves) and employee stock options**	0	0	0	0	0	0
资产Credit	0	0	0	0	0	0
负债Debit	0	0	0	0	0	0
其他投资 **Other investment**	−27	40	2	−276	−437	−205
资产Assets	−38	−3	−13	−396	−350	−244
负债Liabilities	12	43	15	120	−86	39
2.2.2 储备资产 **Reserve assets**	−305	−225	−317	−357	−64	−85
其中:外汇储备 **Foreign exchange reserves**	−304	−220	−315	−349	−51	−97
3.净误差与遗漏 **Net errors and omissions**	−98	−178	−155	−223	−187	−178

中国国际收支概览表 （3）

China's Balance of Payments Abridged (3)

项目 / 年份 Item / Year	2000	2001	2002	2003	2004	2005
1.经常账户 Current account	204	174	354	431	689	1 324
贷方Credit	2 725	2 906	3 551	4 825	6 522	8 403
借方Debit	−2 521	−2 732	−3 197	−4 395	−5 833	−7 080
A.货物和服务 Goods and services	288	281	374	358	512	1 246
贷方Credit	2 531	2 721	3 330	4 480	6 074	7 733
借方Debit	−2 243	−2 440	−2 956	−4 121	−5 562	−6 487
a.货物Goods	299	282	377	398	594	1 301
贷方Credit	2 181	2 329	2 868	3 966	5 429	6 949
借方Debit	−1 881	−2 047	−2 491	−3 568	−4 835	−5 647
b.服务Services	−11	−1	−3	−40	−82	−55
贷方Credit	350	392	462	513	645	785
借方Debit	−362	−393	−465	−553	−727	−840
B.初次收入 Primary income	−147	−192	−149	−102	−51	−161
贷方Credit	126	94	83	161	206	393
借方Debit	−272	−286	−233	−263	−257	−554
C.二次收入 Secondary income	63	85	130	174	229	239
贷方Credit	69	91	138	185	243	277
借方Debit	−5	−6	−8	−10	−14	−39
2.资本和金融账户 Capital and financial account	−86	−125	−432	−513	−819	−1 553
2.1 资本账户 Capital account	0	−1	0	0	−1	41
贷方Credit	0	0	0	0	0	42
借方Debit	0	−1	0	0	−1	−1
2.2 金融账户 Financial account	−86	−125	−432	−512	−818	−1 594

单位：亿美元
Unit: USD 100 million

项目 / 年份 Item / Year	2000	2001	2002	2003	2004	2005
资产Credit	−666	−541	−932	−1 212	−1 916	−3 352
负债Debit	580	416	500	699	1 098	1 758
2.2.1 非储备性质的 金融账户 Financial account excluding reserve assets	20	348	323	549	1 082	912
资产Credit	−561	−67	−177	−150	−16	−845
负债Debit	580	416	500	699	1 098	1 758
直接投资 Direct investment	375	374	468	494	601	904
资产Credit	−9	−69	−25	0	−20	−137
负债Debit	384	442	493	495	621	1 041
证券投资 Portfolio investment	−40	−194	−103	114	197	−47
资产Credit	−113	−207	−121	30	65	−262
负债Debit	73	12	18	84	132	214
金融衍生工具 Financial derivatives (other than reserves) and employee stock options	0	0	0	0	0	0
资产Credit	0	0	0	0	0	0
负债Debit	0	0	0	0	0	0
其他投资 Other investment	−315	169	−41	−60	283	56
资产Assets	−439	208	−31	−180	−61	−447
负债Liabilities	123	−39	−10	120	345	502
2.2.2 储备资产 Reserve assets	−105	−473	−755	−1 061	−1 901	−2 506
其中：外汇储备 Foreign exchange reserves	−109	−466	−742	−1 060	−1 904	−2 526
3.净误差与遗漏 Net errors and omissions	−119	−49	78	82	130	229

中国国际收支概览表（4）

China's Balance of Payments Abridged（4）

项目/年份 Item/Year	2006	2007	2008	2009	2010	2011
1.经常账户Current account	2 318	3 532	4 206	2 433	2 378	1 361
贷方Credit	10 779	13 832	16 597	14 006	17 959	22 087
借方Debit	−8 460	−10 300	−12 391	−11 574	−15 581	−20 726
A.货物和服务Goods and services	2 089	3 080	3 488	2 201	2 230	1 819
贷方Credit	9 917	12 571	14 953	12 497	16 039	20 089
借方Debit	−7 828	−9 490	−11 465	−10 296	−13 809	−18 269
a.货物Goods	2 157	3 117	3 599	2 435	2 464	2 287
贷方Credit	8 977	11 316	13 500	11 272	14 864	18 078
借方Debit	−6 820	−8 199	−9 901	−8 836	−12 400	−15 791
b.服务Services	−68	−37	−111	−234	−234	−468
贷方Credit	941	1 254	1 453	1 226	1 175	2 010
借方Debit	−1 008	−1 291	−1 564	−1 460	−1 409	−2 478
B.初次收入Primary income	−51	80	286	−85	−259	−703
贷方Credit	546	835	1 118	1 083	1 424	1 443
借方Debit	−597	−754	−832	−1 168	−1 683	−2 146
C.二次收入Secondary income	281	371	432	317	407	245
贷方Credit	316	426	526	426	495	556
借方Debit	−35	−55	−94	−110	−88	−311
2.资本和金融账户 Capital and financial account	−2 355	−3 665	−4 394	−2 019	−1 849	−1 223
2.1 资本账户Capital account	40	31	31	39	46	54
贷方Credit	41	33	33	42	48	56
借方Debit	−1	−2	−3	−3	−2	−2
2.2 金融账户Financial account	−2 395	−3 696	−4 425	−2 058	−1 895	−1 278

单位：亿美元
Unit: USD 100 million

项目 / 年份 Item / Year	2006	2007	2008	2009	2010	2011
资产Credit	−4 519	−6 371	−6 087	−4 283	−6 536	−6 136
负债Debit	2 124	2 676	1 662	2 225	4 641	4 858
2.2.1 非储备性质的金融账户 Financial account excluding reserve assets	453	911	371	1 945	2 822	2 600
资产Credit	−1 671	−1 764	−1 291	−280	−1 819	−2 258
负债Debit	2 124	2 676	1 662	2 225	4 641	4 858
直接投资Direct investment	1 001	1 391	1 148	872	1 857	2 317
资产Credit	−239	−172	−567	−439	−580	−484
负债Debit	1 241	1 562	1 715	1 311	2 437	2 801
证券投资Portfolio investment	−684	164	349	271	240	196
资产Credit	−1 113	−45	252	−25	−76	62
负债Debit	429	210	97	296	317	134
金融衍生工具 Financial derivatives (other than reserves) and employee stock options	0	0	0	0	0	0
资产Credit	0	0	0	0	0	0
负债Debit	0	0	0	0	0	0
其他投资Other investment	136	−644	−1 126	803	724	87
资产Assets	−319	−1 548	−976	184	−1 163	−1 836
负债Liabilities	455	904	−150	619	1 887	1 923
2.2.2 储备资产Reserve assets	−2 848	−4 607	−4 795	−4 003	−4 717	−3 878
其中：外汇储备 Foreign exchange reserves	−2 853	−4 609	−4 783	−3 821	−4 696	−3 848
3.净误差与遗漏 Net errors and omissions	36	133	188	−414	−529	−138

中国国际收支概览表（5）

China's Balance of Payments Abridged (5)

项目 / 年份 Item / Year	2012	2013	2014	2015	2016	2017H1
1.经常账户 **Current account**	2 154	1 482	2 774	3 306	1 964	693
贷方Credit	23 933	25 927	28 047	26 930	24 546	12 680
借方Debit	−21 779	−24 445	−25 273	−23 624	−22 583	−11 987
A.货物和服务 **Goods and services**	2 318	2 354	2 627	3 846	2 499	793
贷方Credit	21 751	23 556	25 242	24 293	21 979	11 283
借方Debit	−19 432	−21 202	−22 616	−20 447	−19 480	−10 490
a.货物Goods	3 116	3 590	4 350	5 670	4 941	2 144
贷方Credit	19 735	21 486	22 438	21 428	19 895	10 269
借方Debit	−16 619	−17 896	−18 087	−15 758	−14 954	−8 126
b.服务Services	−797	−1 236	−1 724	−1 824	−2 442	−1 351
贷方Credit	2 016	2 070	2 805	2 865	2 084	1 014
借方Debit	−2 813	−3 306	−4 528	−4 689	−4 526	−2 364
B.初次收入 **Primary income**	−199	−784	133	−454	−440	−34
贷方Credit	1 670	1 840	2 394	2 278	2 258	1 250
借方Debit	−1 869	−2 624	−2 261	−2 732	−2 698	−1 284
C.二次收入 **Secondary income**	34	−87	14	−87	−95	−67
贷方Credit	512	532	411	359	309	147
借方Debit	−477	−619	−397	−446	−404	−213
2.资本和金融账户 **Capital and financial account**	−1 283	−853	−1 692	−1 424	263	389
2.1 资本账户 **Capital account**	43	31	0	3	−3	−1
贷方Credit	45	45	19	5	3	1
借方Debit	−3	−14	−20	−2	−7	−2

单位：亿美元
Unit: USD 100 million

项目 / 年份 Item / Year	2012	2013	2014	2015	2016	2017H1
2.2 金融账户 Financial account	-1 326	-883	-1 691	-1 427	267	390
资产Credit	-3 996	-6 517	-5 806	-491	-2 174	-1 632
负债Debit	2 670	5 633	4 115	-936	2 441	2 021
2.2.1 非储备性质的金融账户 Financial account excluding reserve assets	-360	3 430	-514	-4 856	-4 170	679
资产Credit	-3 030	-2 203	-4 629	-3 920	-6 611	-1 342
负债Debit	2 670	5 633	4 115	-936	2 441	2 021
直接投资 Direct investment	1 763	2 180	1 450	621	-466	139
资产Credit	-650	-730	-1 231	-1 878	-2 172	-411
负债Debit	2 412	2 909	2 681	2 499	1 706	550
证券投资 Portfolio investment	478	529	824	-665	-622	-195
资产Credit	-64	-54	-108	-732	-1 034	-401
负债Debit	542	582	932	67	412	206
金融衍生工具 Financial derivatives (other than reserves) and employee stock options	0	0	0	-21	-47	3
资产Credit	0	0	0	-34	-69	5
负债Debit	0	0	0	13	22	-2
其他投资 Other investment	-2 601	722	-2 788	-4 791	-3 035	732
资产Assets	-2 317	-1 420	-3 289	-1 276	-3 336	-536
负债Liabilities	-284	2 142	502	-3 515	301	1 267
2.2.2 储备资产 Reserve assets	-966	-4 314	-1 178	3 429	4 437	-290
其中:外汇储备 Foreign exchange reserves	-987	-4 327	-1 188	3 423	4 487	-294
3.净误差与遗漏 Net errors and omissions	-871	-629	-1 083	-1 882	-2 227	-1 081

2017年上半年中国国际收支平衡表

China's Balance of Payments in the First Half of 2017

项目	行次	2017H1
1. 经常账户Current account	1	693
贷方Credit	2	12 680
借方Debit	3	−11 987
1.A 货物和服务Goods and services	4	793
贷方Credit	5	11 283
借方Debit	6	−10 490
1.A.a 货物Goods	7	2 144
贷方Credit	8	10 269
借方Debit	9	−8 126
1.A.b 服务Services	10	−1 351
贷方Credit	11	1 014
借方Debit	12	−2 364
1.A.b.1 加工服务Manufacturing services on physical inputs owned by others	13	87
贷方Credit	14	88
借方Debit	15	−1
1.A.b.2 维护和维修服务 Maintenance and repair services n.i.e	16	18
贷方Credit	17	28
借方Debit	18	−10
1.A.b.3 运输Transport	19	−262
贷方Credit	20	173
借方Debit	21	−435
1.A.b.4 旅行Travel	22	−1 159
贷方Credit	23	188
借方Debit	24	−1 347
1.A.b.5 建设Construction	25	10
贷方Credit	26	53
借方Debit	27	−42
1.A.b.6 保险和养老金服务 Insurance and pension services	28	−33
贷方Credit	29	18

单位：亿美元
Unit: USD 100 million

项目	行次	2017H1
借方Debit	30	−51
1.A.b.7 金融服务Financial services	31	8
贷方Credit	32	14
借方Debit	33	−7
1.A.b.8 知识产权使用费 Charges for the use of intellectual property	34	−121
贷方Credit	35	22
借方Debit	36	−143
1.A.b.9 电信、计算机和信息服务 Telecommunications, computer, and information services	37	45
贷方Credit	38	136
借方Debit	39	−91
1.A.b.10 其他商业服务 Other business services	40	76
贷方Credit	41	282
借方Debit	42	−206
1.A.b.11 个人、文化和娱乐服务 Personal, cultural, and recreational services	43	−9
贷方Credit	44	4
借方Debit	45	−12
1.A.b.12 别处未提及的政府服务 Government goods and services n.i.e	46	−11
贷方Credit	47	8
借方Debit	48	−19
1.B 初次收入Primary income	49	−34
贷方Credit	50	1 250
借方Debit	51	−1 284
1.B.1 雇员报酬Compensation of employees	52	85
贷方Credit	53	117
借方Debit	54	−32
1.B.2 投资收益Investment income	55	−122
贷方Credit	56	1 130

2017年上半年中国国际收支平衡表

China's Balance of Payments in the First Half of 2017

项目	行次	2017H1
借方Debit	57	−1 252
1.B.3 其他初次收入Other primary income	58	2
贷方Credit	59	3
借方Debit	60	−1
1.C 二次收入Secondary income	61	−67
贷方Credit	62	147
借方Debit	63	−213
2.资本和金融账户Capital and financial account	64	389
2.1资本账户Capital account	65	−1
贷方Credit	66	1
借方Debit	67	−2
2.2 金融账户Financial account	68	390
资产Assets	69	−1 632
负债Liabilities	70	2 021
2.2.1 非储备性质的金融账户 Financial account excluding reserve assets	71	679
资产Assets	72	−1 342
负债Liabilities	73	2 021
2.2.1.1 直接投资Direct investment	74	139
2.2.1.1.1 直接投资资产Assets	75	−411
2.2.1.1.1.1 股权 Equity and investment fund shares	76	−419
2.2.1.1.1.2 关联企业债务 Debt instruments	77	8
2.2.1.1.2直接投资负债Liabilities	78	550
2.2.1.1.2.1 股权 Equity and investment fund shares	79	520
2.2.1.1.2.2 关联企业债务 Debt instruments	80	30
2.2.1.2 证券投资Portfolio investmen	81	−195
2.2.1.2.1 资产Assets	82	−401
2.2.1.2.1.1 股权Equity and investment fund shares	83	−142
2.2.1.2.1.2 债券Debt securities	84	−259
2.2.1.2.2 负债Liabilities	85	206
2.2.1.2.2.1 股权 Equity and investment fund shares	86	116

单位：亿美元
Unit: USD 100 million

项目	行次	2017H1
2.2.1.2.2.2 债券Debt securities	87	90
2.2.1.3 金融衍生工具 Financial derivatives (other than reserves) and employee stock options	88	3
2.2.1.3.1 资产Assets	89	5
2.2.1.3.2 负债Liabilities	90	−2
2.2.1.4 其他投资Other investment	91	732
2.2.1.4.1 资产Assets	92	−536
2.2.1.4.1.1 其他股权Other equity	93	−1
2.2.1.4.1.2 货币和存款 Currency and deposits	94	−83
2.2.1.4.1.3 贷款Loans	95	−665
2.2.1.4.1.4 保险和养老金 Insurance, pension, and standardized guarantee schemes	96	−3
2.2.1.4.1.5 贸易信贷 Trade credit and advances	97	296
2.2.1.4.1.6 其他应收款 Other accounts receivable	98	−80
2.2.1.4.2 负债Liabilities	99	1 267
2.2.1.4.2.1 其他股权Other equity	100	0
2.2.1.4.2.2 货币和存款 Currency and deposits	101	995
2.2.1.4.2.3 贷款Loans	102	547
2.2.1.4.2.4 保险和养老金 Insurance, pension, and standardized guarantee schemes	103	2
2.2.1.4.2.5 贸易信贷 Trade credit and advances	104	−339
2.2.1.4.2.6 其他应付款 Other accounts payable	105	62
2.2.1.4.2.7 特别提款权 Special drawing rights	106	0
2.2.2 储备资产Reserve assets	107	−290
2.2.2.1 货币黄金Monetary gold	108	0
2.2.2.2 特别提款权 Special drawing rights	109	0
2.2.2.3 在国际货币基金组织的储备头寸 Reserve position in the IMF	110	4
2.2.2.4 外汇储备 Foreign exchange reserves	111	−294
2.2.2.5其他储备资产 Other reserve assets	112	0
3.净误差与遗漏Net errors and omissions	113	−1 081

中国国际投资头寸表

China's International Investment Position

项目	2009年末	2010年末	2011年末	2012年末	2013年末	2014年末	2015年末	2016年	2017年上半年末
净头寸Net International Investment Position	14 905	16 880	16 884	18 665	19 960	16 028	15 965	18 005	17 515
A.资产 Assets	34 369	41 189	47 345	52 132	59 861	64 383	62 189	64 666	66 446
1.直接投资 Direct investment	2 458	3 172	4 248	5 319	6 605	8 826	11 293	13 172	13 697
1.1股权Equity and investment fund shares	—	—	—	—	—	7 408	9 393	10650	11 178
1.2 关联企业债务 Debt instruments	—	—	—	—	—	1 418	1 901	2 522	2 519
2.证券投资 Portfolio investment	2 428	2 571	2 044	2 406	2 585	2 625	2 613	3 651	4 143
2.1股权 Equity and investment fund shares	546	630	864	1 298	1 530	1 613	1 620	2 149	2 546
2.2 债券Debt securities	1 882	1 941	1 180	1 108	1 055	1 012	993	1 502	1 597
3.金融衍生工具 Financial derivatives (other than reserves) and employee stock options	—	—	—	—	—	0	36	52	60
4.其他投资 Other investment	4 952	6 304	8 495	10 527	11 867	13 938	14 185	16 811	17 042
4.1 其他股权 Other equity	—	—	—	—	—	0	1	1	55
4.2 货币和存款 Currency and deposits	1 310	2 051	2942	3 906	3 751	4 453	3 895	3 816	3 816
4.3 贷款Loans	974	1 174	2 232	2 778	3 089	3 747	4 569	5 622	6 373
4.4 保险和养老金Insurance, pension, and standardized guarantee schemes	—	—	—	—	—	0	172	123	105
4.5 贸易信贷 Trade credit and advances	1 444	2 060	2 769	3 387	3 990	4 677	5 137	6 145	5 849
4.6 其他 Other accounts receivable	1 224	1 018	552	457	1 038	1 061	412	1 105	844
5.储备资产Reserve assets	24 532	29 142	32 558	33 879	38 804	38 993	34 061	30 978	31 504
5.1货币黄金 Monetary gold	371	481	530	567	408	401	602	679	736
5.2 特别提款权 Special drawing rights	125	123	119	114	112	105	103	97	100

单位：亿美元
Unit: USD 100 million

项目	2009年末	2010年末	2011年末	2012年末	2013年末	2014年末	2015年末	2016年	2017年上半年末
5.3 在国际货币基金组织的储备头寸 Reserve position in the IMF	44	64	98	82	71	57	45	96	95
5.4 外汇储备 Foreign currency reserves	23 992	28 473	31 811	33 116	38 213	38 430	33 304	30 105	30 568
5.5 其他储备资产 Other reserve assets	—	—	—	—	—	0	7	2	5
B.负债 Liabilities	**19 464**	**24 308**	**30 461**	**33 467**	**39 901**	**48 355**	**46 225**	**46 660**	**48 931**
1.直接投资 Direct investment	**13 148**	**15 696**	**19 069**	**20 680**	**23 312**	**25 991**	**28 423**	**28 659**	**29 245**
1.1 股权Equity and investment fund shares	—	—	—	—	—	24 076	26 181	26 543	27 078
1.2关联企业债务 Debt instruments	—	—	—	—	—	1 915	2 242	2 117	2 167
2.证券投资 Portfolio investment	**1 900**	**2 239**	**2 485**	**3 361**	**3 865**	**7 962**	**8 105**	**8 086**	**8 583**
2.1 股权Equity and investment fund shares	1 748	2 061	2 114	2 619	2 977	6 513	5 906	5 927	6 221
2.2 债券Debt securities	152	178	371	742	889	1 449	2 200	2 159	2 362
3. 金融衍生工具Financial derivatives (other than reserves) and employee stock options	**—**	**—**	**—**	**—**	**—**	**0**	**53**	**66**	**49**
4.其他投资 Other investment	**4 416**	**6 373**	**8 907**	**9 426**	**12 724**	**14 402**	**9 643**	**9 849**	**11 054**
4.1 其他股权 Other equity	—	—	—	—	—	0	—	0	0
4.2 货币和存款 Currency and deposits	937	1 650	2 477	2 446	3 466	5 030	3 267	3 156	4 177
4.3 贷款Loans	1 636	2 389	3 724	3 680	5 642	5 720	3 293	3 236	3 910
4.4 保险和养老金 Insurance, pension, and standardized guarantee schemes	—	—	—	—	—	0	93	88	95
4.5 贸易信贷 Trade credit and advances	1 617	2 112	2 492	2 915	3 365	3 344	2 721	2 883	2 544
4.6 其他 Other accounts payable	121	106	106	277	144	207	172	391	232
4.7 特别提款权 Special drawing rights	106	116	107	107	108	101	97	94	97

外汇储备

Foreign Exchange Reserves

单位：亿美元
Unit: USD 100 million

年份 year	外汇储备余额 Foreign Exchange Reserves	外汇储备增加额 Increase of Foreign Exchange Reserves
1990	111	55
1991	217	106
1992	194	−23
1993	212	18
1994	516	304
1995	736	220
1996	1 050	315
1997	1 399	348
1998	1 450	51
1999	1 547	97
2000	1 656	109
2001	2 122	466
2002	2 864	742
2003	4 033	1 168
2004	6 099	2 067
2005	8 189	2 090
2006	10 663	2 475
2007	15 282	4 619
2008	19 460	4 178
2009	23 992	4 531
2010	28 473	4 481
2011	31 811	3 338
2012	33 116	1 304
2013	38 213	5 097
2014	38 430	217
2015	33 304	−5 127
2016	30 105	−3 198
2017H1	30 568	463

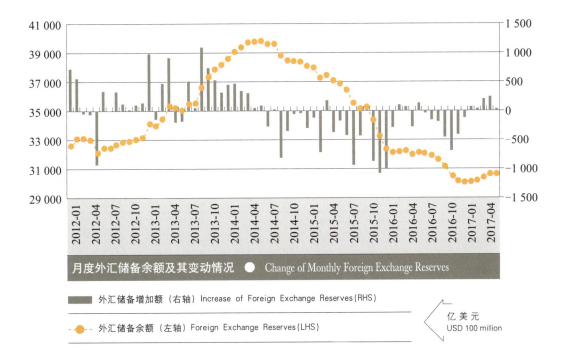

月度外汇储备余额及其变动情况 ● Change of Monthly Foreign Exchange Reserves

外汇储备增加额（右轴）Increase of Foreign Exchange Reserves（RHS）

外汇储备余额（左轴）Foreign Exchange Reserves（LHS）

亿 美 元
USD 100 million

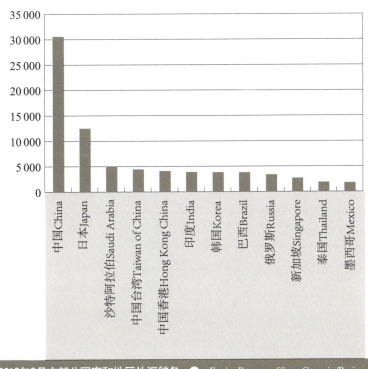

2016年6月末部分国家和地区外汇储备 ● Foreign Reserves of Some Countries/Regions, End−2016H1

亿 美 元
USD 100 million

二、对外贸易①

II. Foreign Trade

2016年世界货物贸易出口前十名

Top 10 Countries/Regions of Goods Export in 2016

国家/地区 Countries/Regions	出口额（10亿美元） Export（USD billions）	增长 Increase（%）	占世界出口总额比重 Ratio to total Export of the world（%）	2016年排名 Ranking in 2016
世界World	15 955	−3	100	
1.中国P.R.C	2 098	−8	13.2	1
2.美国U.S.A	1 455	−3	9.1	2
3.德国Germany	1 340	1	8.4	3
4.日本Japan	645	3	4	4
5.荷兰Netherlands	570	0	3.6	5
6.中国香港HongKong,SAR	517	1	3.2	7
7.法国France	501	−1	3.1	8
8.韩国Korea	495	−6	3.1	6
9.意大利Italy	465	1	2.9	10
10.英国UK	409	−1.1	2.6	9

① 数据来源：海关总署；世界贸易组织。

Sources: General Administration of Customs; World Trade Organization.

2016年世界货物贸易进口前十名

Top 10 Countries/Regions of Goods Import in 2016

国家/地区 Countries/Regions	进口额（10亿美元） Import（USD billions）	增长 Increase（%）	占世界进口总额比重 Ratio to total Import of the world（%）	2016年排名 Ranking in 2016
世界World	16 225	−3	100	
1.美国U.S.A	2 551	−3	13.9	1
2.中国P.R.C	1 587	−5	9.8	2
3.德国Germany	1 055	−0	6.5	3
4.英国UK	636	1	3.9	5
5.日本Japan	607	−6	3.7	4
6.法国France	573	0	3.5	6
7.中国香港HongKong,SAR	547	−2	3.4	7
8.荷兰Netherlands	503	−2	3.4	8
9.加拿大Canada	417	−5	2.6	10
10.韩国Korea	406	−7	2.5	9

中国进出口总值

单位：亿美元
Unit: USD 100 million

China's Total Value of Import & Export

年度 Year	进出口 Import & Export	出口 Export	进口 Import	差额 Balance
1981	440	220	220	0
1982	416	223	193	30
1983	436	222	214	8
1984	535	261	274	−13
1985	696	274	423	−149
1986	738	309	429	−120
1987	827	394	432	−38
1988	1 028	475	553	−78
1989	1 117	525	591	−66
1990	1 154	621	534	87
1991	1 357	719	638	81
1992	1 655	849	806	44
1993	1 957	917	1 040	−122
1994	2 366	1 210	1 156	54
1995	2 809	1 488	1 321	167
1996	2 899	1 511	1 388	122
1997	3 252	1 828	1 424	404
1998	3 239	1 837	1 402	435
1999	3 606	1 949	1 657	292
2000	4 743	2 492	2 251	241
2001	5 097	2 661	2 436	225
2002	6 208	3 256	2 952	304
2003	8 510	4 382	4 128	255
2004	11 546	5 933	5 612	321
2005	14 219	7 620	6 600	1 020
2006	17 604	9 689	7 915	1 775
2007	21 746	12 186	9 560	2 627
2008	25 633	14 307	11 326	2 981
2009	22 075	12 016	10 059	1 957
2010	29 740	15 778	13 962	1 815
2011	36 419	18 984	17 435	1 549
2012	38 671	20 487	18 184	2 303
2013	41 590	22 090	19 500	2 590
2014	43 015	23 423	19 592	3 831
2015	39 530	22 735	16 796	5 939
2016	36 856	20 976	15 879	5 097
2017H1	19 095	10 473	8 623	1 850

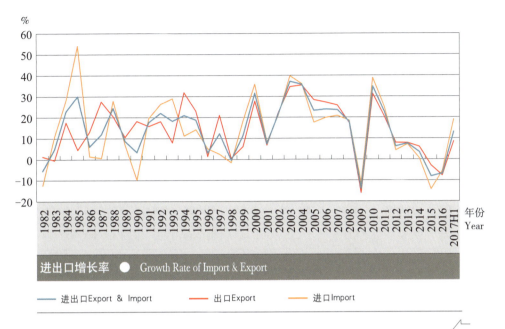

进出口增长率 ● Growth Rate of Import & Export

—— 进出口Export ＆ Import　　—— 出口Export　　—— 进口Import

增长率 (%)
Growth Rate (%)

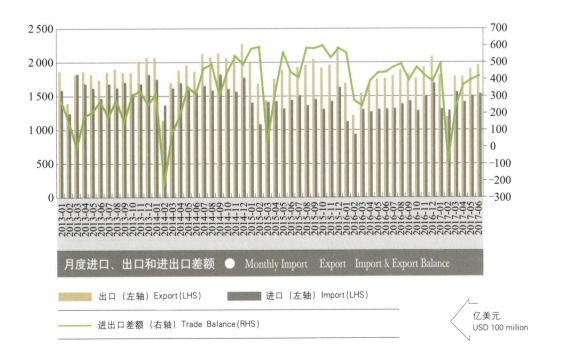

月度进口、出口和进出口差额 ● Monthly Import　Export　Import & Export Balance

▮ 出口（左轴）Export(LHS)　　▮ 进口（左轴）Import(LHS)

—— 进出口差额（右轴）Trade Balance(RHS)

亿美元
USD 100 million

按贸易方式分类进出口

Import & Export by Trading Forms

贸易方式Trading Forms	2007	2008	2009	2010	2011	2012	2013	2014	2015	2016	2017H1
进口Import	**955 818**	**1 133 086**	**1 005 555**	**1 394 829**	**1 743 458**	**1 817 826**	**1 950 289**	**1 960 290**	**1 681 951**	**1 587 921**	**862 277**
一般贸易Ordinary Trade	428 648	572 677	533 872	767 978	1 007 464	1 021 819	1 109 718	1 109 513	923 188	899 013	515 853
国家间、国际组织间无偿援助和捐赠的物资 Foreign Aid and Donation by Overseas	35	49	43	22	16	27	21	38	15	19	2
其他捐赠物资 Other Donations	10	58	136	185	266	338	11	10	48	8	3
来料加工装配贸易 Processing and Assembling Trade	89 165	90 162	75 993	99 295	93 635	84 459	87 543	97 537	91 569	85 261	44 623
进料加工贸易 Processing with Imported Materials	279 228	288 243	246 345	318 134	376 161	396 710	409 447	426 843	355 434	311 432	151 461
寄售代销贸易 Goods on Consignment	2	2	2	2	2	1	0	0		0	2
边境小额贸易 Border trade	7 589	8 975	7 196	9 634	14 448	15 289	14 065	9 856	7 160	7 019	4 382
加工贸易进口设备 Equipment Imported for Processing & Assembling	3 277	2 859	953	1 212	885	912	969	687	635	463	293
租赁贸易 Goods on Lease	8 280	6 932	3 448	5 628	5 459	6 760	8 656	10 212	9 041	2 860	1 283
外商投资企业作为投资进口的设备物品 Equipment or Materials Imported as Investment by Foreign-invested Enterprises	25 906	27 677	15 176	16 312	17 508	13 429	9 835	9 059	6 161	4 067	1 864
出料加工贸易 Outward Processing Trade	39	160	78	126	73	236	252	307	300	265	125
易货贸易 Barter Trade	4	1	8	1	2	0	1	3	3	8	38
免税外汇商品 Duty Free Commodities on Payment of Foreign Exchange	6	6	5	10	13	26	28	20	15	22	9
保税监管场所进出境货物 Customs Warehousing Trade	41 720	57 277	54 392	61 099	79 658	83 969	84 844	99 870	88 705	96 773	57 256
海关特殊监管区域物流货物 Entrepot Trade by Bonded Area	66 910	73 739	64 259	109 241	140 831	185 132	218 448	186 689	182 004	158 044	73 548
海关特殊监管区域进口设备 Equipment Imported into Export Processing Zone	4 108	3 118	2 113	3 994	4 741	6 094	3 993	5 133	6 544	4 894	3 487
其他 Others	890	1 150	1 535	1 957	2 296	2 624	2 458	2 950	9 510	15 542	7 167

单位：百万美元
Unit: USD million

贸易方式Trading Forms	2007	2008	2009	2010	2011	2012	2013	2014	2015	2016	2017H1
出口Export	1 218 015	1 428 546	1 201 663	1 577 932	1 898 600	2 048 935	2 210 042	2 342 747	2 274 950	2 097 637	1 047 273
一般贸易 Ordinary Trade	538 576	662 584	529 833	720 733	917 124	988 007	1 087 553	1 203 682	1 215 697	1 131 043	567 848
国家间、国际组织间无偿援助和捐赠的物资 Foreign Aid and Donation by overseas	201	231	291	294	471	551	456	478	493	472	187
其他捐赠物资 Other Donations	0	2	8	3	11	2	8	6	6	6	2
补偿贸易 Compensation Trade	0	0	0	0	0	0	0	0	0	0	0
来料加工装配贸易 Processing and Assembling Trade	116 043	110 520	93 423	112 317	107 653	98 866	92 479	90 692	84 097	76 040	38 497
进料加工贸易 Processing with Imported Materials	501 613	564 663	493 558	628 017	727 763	763 913	768 337	793 668	713 692	639 557	307 533
寄售代销贸易 Goods on Consignment	4	4	6	1	2	4	1	0	0	0	0
边境小额贸易 Border trade	13 739	21 904	13 667	16 408	20 203	24 216	30 929	37 207	30 465	26 407	12 938
对外承包工程出口货物 Contracting Projects	5 188	10 963	13 357	12 617	14 923	14 782	16 011	16 326	16 132	13 304	7 302
租赁贸易 Goods on Lease	84	189	117	145	166	562	305	327	265	192	94
出料加工贸易 Outward Processing Trade	44	118	46	185	198	196	199	235	205	221	91
易货贸易 Barter Trade	48	16	1	1	1	1	2	3	2	2	15
保税监管场所进出境货物 Customs Warehousing Trade	18 624	28 404	26 793	35 366	43 294	42 477	46 510	53 288	49 246	38 408	18 594
海关特殊监管区域物流货物 Entrepot Trade by Bonded Area	20 977	23 937	21 476	36 502	49 655	94 819	141 990	110 395	109 580	94 289	41 776
其他 Others	2 916	5 011	9 088	15 343	17 135	20 540	25 262	36 438	55 069	78 212	52 395

按企业类型分类进出口

单位：亿美元
Unit: USD 100 million

Import & Export by Type of Enterprises

企业类型Type of Enterprises	2007	2008	2009	2010	2011	2012	2013	2014	2015	2016	2017H1
进口Import	**9 558**	**11 331**	**10 056**	**13 948**	**17 435**	**18 178**	**19 503**	**19 603**	**16 820**	**15 879**	**8 623**
国有企业State-owned Enterprises	2 697	3 538	2 885	3 876	4 934	4 954	4 990	4 911	4 078	3 608	2 169
外商投资企业 Foreign-funded Enterprises	5 594	6 200	5 452	7 380	8 648	8 712	8 748	9 093	8 299	7 705	3 982
中外合作 Sino-foreign Contractual Joint Ventures	88	88	66	74	86	82	83	87	62	43	23
中外合资 Sino-foreign Equity Joint Ventures	1 549	1 818	1 586	2 095	2 561	2 748	2 842	2 858	2 461	2 238	1 142
外商独资 Foreign Investment Enterprises	3 957	4 294	3 799	5 212	6 002	5 883	5 823	6 149	5 776	5 424	2 818
集体企业/私营企业① Collective Enterprises/Private owned Enterprises	232	289	265	349	407	353	4 368	4 475	4 116	4 179	2 271
其他Other Enterprises	1 035	1 304	1 454	2 343	3 445	4 158	1 397	1 124	326	375	200
出口Export	**12 180**	**14 285**	**12 017**	**15 779**	**18 986**	**20 489**	**22 100**	**23 427**	**22 749**	**20 976**	**10 473**
国有企业State-owned Enterprises	2 248	2 572	1 910	2 344	2 672	2 563	2 490	2 565	2 424	2 156	1 104
外商投资企业 Foreign-funded Enterprises	6 955	7 906	6 722	8 623	9 953	10 227	10 443	10 747	10 047	9 169	4 469
中外合作 Sino-foreign Contractual Joint Ventures	181	183	146	165	177	162	157	136	114	99	43
中外合资 Sino-foreign Equity Joint Ventures	1 988	2 269	1 824	2 376	2 731	2 873	3 009	3 055	2 825	2 542	1 223
外商独资 Foreign Investment Enterprises	4 786	5 454	4 752	6 082	7 046	7 193	7 277	7 556	7 109	6 529	3 203
集体企业/私营企业 Collective Enterprises/Private owned Enterprises	469	547	405	499	554	509	8 633	9 547	9 738	9 148	4 657
其他Other Enterprises	2 508	3 260	2 979	4 314	5 807	7 190	534	958	541	503	242
差额Balance	**2 622**	**2 955**	**1 961**	**1 831**	**1 551**	**2 311**	**2 598**	**3 825**	**5 930**	**5 097**	**1 850**
国有企业State-owned Enterprises	−449	−966	−975	−1 532	−2 262	−2 391	−2 500	−2 346	−1 654	−1 452	−1 065
外商投资企业 Foreign-funded Enterprises	1 361	1 706	1 270	1 243	1 305	1 515	1 695	1 654	1 748	1 465	487
中外合作 Sino-foreign Contractual Joint Ventures	93	95	80	91	91	80	74	49	52	56	21
中外合资 Sino-foreign Equity Joint Ventures	439	451	238	281	170	125	167	197	364	304	81
外商独资 Foreign Investment Enterprises	829	1 160	953	870	1 044	1 310	1 454	1 407	1 333	1 105	385
集体企业/私营企业 Collective Enterprises/Private owned Enterprises	237	258	140	150	147	156	4 265	5 072	5 622	4 968	2 386
其他Other Enterprises	1 473	1 956	1 525	1 971	2 362	3 032	−863	−166	214	128	42

① 2013 年该项下的数据由集体企业调整为私营企业。Data of Collective Enterprises was replaced by that of Private Owned Enterprises from 2013.

2017上半年按贸易方式分类的进口构成
Components of Import by Trading Forms in the First Half of 2017

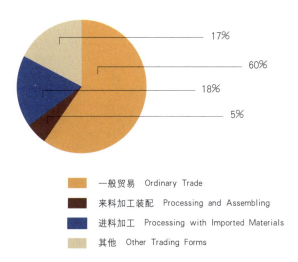

17%
60%
18%
5%

■ 一般贸易 Ordinary Trade
■ 来料加工装配 Processing and Assembling
■ 进料加工 Processing with Imported Materials
■ 其他 Other Trading Forms

2017上半年按贸易方式分类的出口构成
Components of Export by Trading Forms in the First Half of 2017

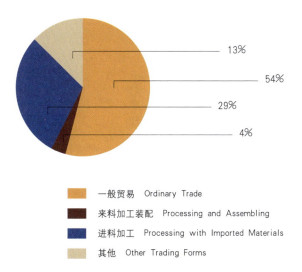

13%
54%
29%
4%

■ 一般贸易 Ordinary Trade
■ 来料加工装配 Processing and Assembling
■ 进料加工 Processing with Imported Materials
■ 其他 Other Trading Forms

2017上半年按企业类型分类的进口构成
Components of Import by Type of Enterprises in the First Half of 2017

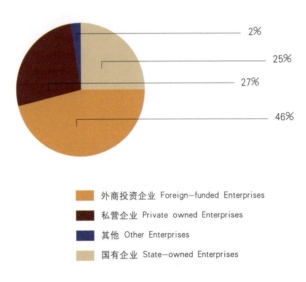

2% \
25% \
27% \
46%

■ 外商投资企业 Foreign-funded Enterprises
■ 私营企业 Private owned Enterprises
■ 其他 Other Enterprises
□ 国有企业 State-owned Enterprises

2017上半年按企业类型分类的出口构成
Components of Export by Type of Enterprises in the First Half of 2017

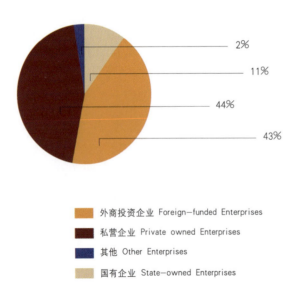

2% \
11% \
44% \
43%

■ 外商投资企业 Foreign-funded Enterprises
■ 私营企业 Private owned Enterprises
■ 其他 Other Enterprises
□ 国有企业 State-owned Enterprises

2017上半年进出口按贸易方式分类

单位：亿美元
Unit: USD 100 million

Import & Export by Trading Forms in the First Half of 2017

贸易方式 Trading Forms	进口 Import 金额 Value	同比（%）Increase	出口 Export 金额 Value	同比（%）Increase	进出口差额 Import & Export Balance
总值 **Total Value**	**8 623**	**18.9**	**10 473**	**8.5**	**1 850**
一般贸易 Ordinary Trade	5159	23.1	5678	6.4	520
加工贸易 Processing Trade	1 961	12.0	3 460	8.0	1 499
来料加工装配 Processing and Assembling	446	16.6	385	14.8	−61
进料加工 Processing with imported materials	1 515	11.0	3 075	7.5	1 561
其他贸易 Other trading forms	1 503	11.8	1 334	14.9	−169

2017上半年进出口按企业类型分类

Import & Export by Type of Enterprises in the First Half of 2017

企业类型 Type of Enterprises	进口 Import		出口 Export		进出口差额
	金额Value	同比（％）Increase	金额Value	同比（％）Increase	Import & Export Balance
总值 Total Value	8 623	18.9	10 473	8.5	1 850
国有企业 State-owned Enterprises	2 169	33.5	1 104	6.7	-1 065
外资企业 Foreign-funded Enterprises	3 982	11.9	4 469	6.2	487
私营和其他企业 Private Owned and other Enterprises	2 471	18.2	4 899	6.8	2 428

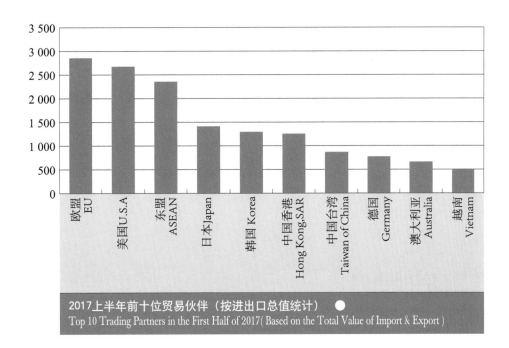

2017上半年前十位贸易伙伴（按进出口总值统计） ●
Top 10 Trading Partners in the First Half of 2017(Based on the Total Value of Import & Export)

亿 美 元
USD 100 million

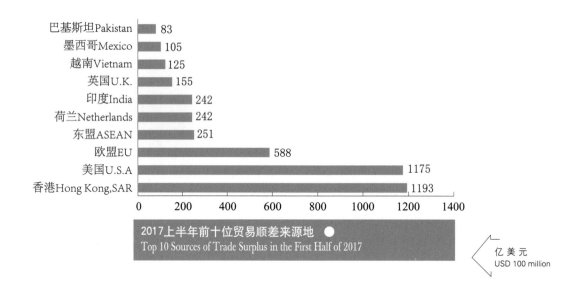

2017上半年前十位贸易顺差来源地 ●
Top 10 Sources of Trade Surplus in the First Half of 2017

亿 美 元
USD 100 million

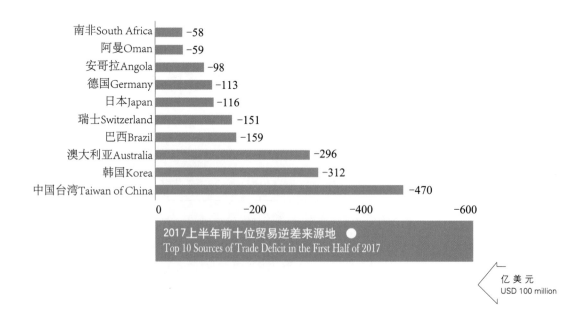

2017上半年前十位贸易逆差来源地 ●
Top 10 Sources of Trade Deficit in the First Half of 2017

亿 美 元
USD 100 million

三、外汇市场和人民币汇率[①]

Ⅲ．Foreign Exchange Market and Exchange Rate of Renminbi

人民币对美元交易中间价月平均汇价

人民币元/100美元
RMB per 100 USD

Monthly Average Transaction Mid Rates of Renminbi against US dollar，1980—2017

年份Year 月份Month	1980	1981	1982	1983	1984	1985	1986	1987	1988	1989	1990
1月/Jan.	149.37	154.87	176.77	192.01	204.12	280.88	320.15	372.21	372.21	372.21	472.21
2月/Feb.	150.05	161.06	181.74	196.03	205.72	282.51	320.70	372.21	372.21	372.21	472.21
3月/Mar.	155.12	162.80	183.79	197.80	206.08	284.51	321.20	372.21	372.21	372.21	472.21
4月/Apr.	155.70	166.20	185.19	198.72	208.91	284.11	320.61	372.21	372.21	372.21	472.21
5月/May	149.06	172.27	180.97	198.52	218.21	284.75	319.44	372.21	372.21	372.21	472.21
6月/Jun.	146.50	176.05	189.70	198.95	221.22	286.25	320.35	372.21	372.21	372.21	472.21
7月/Jul.	145.25	175.98	192.36	198.88	229.39	287.38	363.82	372.21	372.21	372.21	472.21
8月/Aug.	147.26	179.52	193.87	198.00	236.43	290.23	370.36	372.21	372.21	372.21	472.21
9月/Sept.	146.81	175.01	195.04	198.14	253.26	296.26	370.66	372.21	372.21	372.21	472.21
10月/Oct.	148.03	175.05	198.22	196.17	264.00	306.73	371.64	372.21	372.21	372.21	472.21
11月/Nov.	151.73	173.46	199.41	198.90	266.16	320.15	372.21	372.21	372.21	372.21	495.54
12月/Dec.	154.19	173.78	193.99	198.69	278.91	320.15	372.21	372.21	372.21	423.82	522.21
年平均 Annual Average	149.84	170.50	189.25	197.57	232.70	293.66	345.28	372.21	372.21	376.51	478.32

①资料来源：国家外汇管理局。
Source：State Administration of Foreign Exchange.

人民币对美元交易中间价月平均汇价

人民币元/100美元
RMB per 100 USD

Monthly Average Transaction Mid Rates of Renminbi against US dollar, 1980—2017

月份Month \ 年份Year	1991	1992	1993	1994	1995	1996	1997	1998	1999	2000	2001	2002
1 月/Jan.	522.21	544.81	576.40	870.00	844.13	831.86	829.63	827.91	827.90	827.93	827.71	827.67
2 月/Feb.	522.21	546.35	576.99	870.28	843.54	831.32	829.29	827.91	827.80	827.79	827.70	827.66
3 月/Mar.	522.21	547.34	573.13	870.23	842.76	832.89	829.57	827.92	827.91	827.86	827.76	827.70
4 月/Apr.	526.59	549.65	570.63	869.55	842.25	833.15	829.57	827.92	827.92	827.93	827.71	827.72
5 月/May	531.39	550.36	572.17	866.49	831.28	832.88	829.29	827.90	827.85	827.77	827.72	827.69
6 月/Jun.	535.35	547.51	573.74	865.72	830.08	832.26	829.21	827.97	827.80	827.72	827.71	827.70
7 月/Jul.	535.55	544.32	576.12	864.03	830.07	831.60	829.11	827.98	827.77	827.93	827.69	827.68
8 月/Aug.	537.35	542.87	577.64	858.98	830.75	830.81	828.94	827.99	827.73	827.96	827.70	827.67
9 月/Sept.	537.35	549.48	578.70	854.03	831.88	830.44	828.72	827.89	827.74	827.86	827.68	827.70
10 月/Oct.	537.90	553.69	578.68	852.93	831.55	830.00	828.38	827.78	827.74	827.85	827.68	827.69
11月/Nov.	538.58	561.31	579.47	851.69	831.35	829.93	828.11	827.78	827.82	827.74	827.69	827.71
12月/Dec.	541.31	579.82	580.68	848.45	831.56	829.90	827.96	827.79	827.93	827.72	827.68	827.72
年平均 Annual Average	532.33	551.46	576.20	861.87	835.10	831.42	828.98	827.91	827.83	827.84	827.70	827.70

人民币对美元交易中间价月平均汇价

人民币元/100美元
RMB per 100 USD

Monthly Average Transaction Mid Rates of Renminbi against US dollar, 1980—2017

月份Month 年份Year	2003	2004	2005	2006	2007	2008	2009	2010	2011	2012	2013	2014	2015	2016
1 月/Jan.	827.68	827.69	827.65	806.68	778.98	724.78	683.82	682.73	660.27	631.68	627.87	610.43	612.72	655.27
2 月/Feb.	827.73	827.71	827.65	804.93	775.46	716.01	683.57	682.70	658.31	630.00	628.42	611.28	613.39	653.11
3 月/Mar.	827.72	827.71	827.65	803.50	773.90	707.52	683.41	682.64	656.62	630.81	627.43	613.58	615.07	650.64
4 月/Apr.	827.71	827.69	827.65	801.56	772.47	700.07	683.12	682.62	652.92	629.66	624.71	615.53	613.02	647.62
5 月/May	827.69	827.71	827.65	801.52	767.04	697.24	682.45	682.74	649.88	630.62	619.70	616.36	611.43	653.15
6 月/Jun.	827.71	827.67	827.65	800.67	763.30	689.71	683.32	681.65	647.78	631.78	617.18	615.57	611.61	658.74
7 月/Jul.	827.73	827.67	822.90	799.10	758.05	683.76	683.20	677.75	646.14	632.35	617.25	615.69	611.67	667.74
8 月/Aug.	827.70	827.68	810.19	797.33	757.53	685.15	683.22	679.01	640.9	634.04	617.08	616.06	630.56	664.74
9 月/Sept.	827.71	827.67	809.22	793.68	752.58	683.07	682.89	674.62	638.33	633.95	615.88	615.28	636.91	667.15
10 月/Oct.	827.67	827.65	808.89	790.32	750.12	683.16	682.75	667.32	635.66	631.44	613.93	614.41	634.86	674.42
11月/Nov.	827.69	827.65	808.40	786.52	742.33	682.86	682.74	665.58	634.08	629.53	613.72	614.32	636.66	683.75
12月/Dec.	827.70	827.65	807.59	782.38	736.76	684.24	682.79	665.15	632.81	629.00	611.60	612.38	644.76	691.82
年平均 Annual Average	827.70	827.68	819.42	797.18	760.40	694.51	683.10	676.95	646.14	631.25	619.32	614.28	622.72	664.23

2017年1-6月人民币市场汇率汇总表

林吉特、卢布单位：外币/100人民币
其他9种币种单位：人民币元/100外币
MYR, RUB Unit: foreign currency per 100 RMB
Other 9 Currency unit: RMB per 100 foreign currency

Transaction Mid Rates of Renminbi in the First Half of 2017

月份Month	币种 Currency	期初价 Beginning of Period	期末价 End of Period	最高价 Highest	最低价 Lowest	期平均 Period Average	累计平均 Accumulative Average
1月	美元	694.98	685.88	695.26	683.31	689.18	689.18
	港币	89.586	88.415	89.638	88.093	88.858	88.858
	日元	5.9305	6.0596	6.0702	5.9192	5.9939	5.9939
	欧元	727.72	738.21	738.21	724.69	731.79	731.79
	英镑	854.96	867.56	867.56	829.58	847.94	847.94
	澳元	500.88	520.23	520.28	500.88	512.86	512.86
	新西兰元	482.42	501.08	501.08	481.35	489.02	489.02
	新加坡元	479.88	486.13	486.13	479.30	482.29	482.29
	瑞士法郎	680.34	687.59	687.59	678.42	682.43	682.43
	加元	517.91	525.44	525.44	515.20	521.24	521.24
	林吉特	64.364	64.419	65.103	64.364	64.566	64.566
	卢布	881.49	864.80	881.49	862.16	868.81	868.81
2月	美元	685.56	687.50	688.98	684.56	687.13	688.16
	港币	88.354	88.580	88.806	88.220	88.552	88.705
	日元	6.0781	6.0986	6.1399	6.0020	6.0788	6.0363
	欧元	738.25	727.74	740.10	725.43	730.85	731.32
	英镑	859.24	854.67	862.55	853.31	857.81	852.87
	澳元	524.88	527.58	529.50	524.48	526.94	519.90
	新西兰元	499.72	493.86	503.03	491.84	496.03	492.53
	新加坡元	486.06	489.15	489.30	483.16	485.49	483.89
	瑞士法郎	691.23	680.99	692.13	677.35	685.60	684.01
	加元	526.43	521.24	527.35	521.24	524.37	522.80
	林吉特	64.464	64.391	64.856	64.214	64.499	64.533
	卢布	865.30	845.75	865.30	830.90	847.99	858.40
3月	美元	687.98	689.93	691.25	687.01	689.32	688.61
	港币	88.629	88.779	89.011	88.456	88.764	88.728
	日元	6.0913	6.1766	6.2172	6.0042	6.1043	6.0628
	欧元	726.48	737.21	747.26	723.34	736.68	733.41
	英镑	850.90	861.19	864.18	839.39	850.73	852.04
	澳元	526.29	527.90	533.70	518.90	525.58	522.11
	新西兰元	493.20	482.91	493.20	476.76	483.27	488.92
	新加坡元	489.31	493.65	494.46	486.35	490.58	486.50
	瑞士法郎	683.50	689.78	698.22	680.15	688.01	685.57
	加元	516.91	517.62	517.93	511.76	515.34	519.89
	林吉特	64.349	63.867	64.532	63.867	64.180	64.395
	卢布	848.91	813.15	857.32	813.15	840.25	851.32

2017年1-6月人民币市场汇率汇总表

林吉特、卢布单位：外币/100人民币
其他9种币种单位：人民币元/100外币
MYR, RUB Unit: foreign currency per 100 RMB
Other 9 Currency unit: RMB per 100 foreign currency

Transaction Mid Rates of Renminbi in the First Half of 2017

月份Month	币种 Currency	期初价 Beginning of Period	期末价 End of Period	最高价 Highest	最低价 Lowest	期平均 Period Average	累计平均 Accumulative Average
4月	美元	689.06	689.31	690.42	686.51	688.45	688.57
	港币	88.671	88.584	88.870	88.316	88.557	88.688
	日元	6.2221	6.2023	6.3491	6.1964	6.2655	6.1102
	欧元	736.30	749.45	752.50	730.25	738.29	734.55
	英镑	857.67	889.61	889.61	855.11	870.58	856.37
	澳元	521.87	515.34	522.79	515.34	519.19	521.43
	新西兰元	481.06	474.81	484.83	474.81	480.90	487.04
	新加坡元	492.94	493.90	494.36	490.94	492.78	487.96
	瑞士法郎	688.13	693.82	694.12	684.12	688.42	686.24
	加元	514.62	506.28	519.13	506.28	513.16	518.32
	林吉特	64.117	62.822	64.389	62.822	63.787	64.253
	卢布	813.46	826.93	831.96	810.73	819.98	844.00
5月	美元	689.56	686.33	690.66	686.12	688.27	688.51
	港币	88.653	88.075	88.726	88.075	88.397	88.628
	日元	6.1677	6.1995	6.1995	6.0452	6.1331	6.1149
	欧元	752.27	767.60	773.15	750.16	760.42	739.88
	英镑	889.53	879.85	895.05	879.85	891.04	863.52
	澳元	519.51	512.60	519.78	507.58	512.24	519.53
	新西兰元	477.19	486.84	486.84	471.82	477.47	485.07
	新加坡元	494.03	495.50	496.88	489.12	493.48	489.10
	瑞士法郎	692.71	704.06	707.19	684.73	697.54	688.57
	加元	504.35	510.13	512.88	500.95	506.01	515.78
	林吉特	62.895	62.282	62.997	62.187	62.688	63.930
	卢布	826.73	824.30	845.53	818.11	829.29	840.96
6月	美元	680.90	677.44	682.92	677.44	680.19	686.97
	港币	87.391	86.792	87.565	86.792	87.228	88.369
	日元	6.1526	6.0485	6.2017	6.0476	6.1367	6.1190
	欧元	766.58	774.96	774.96	758.03	763.89	744.32
	英镑	877.00	881.44	881.44	860.86	870.58	864.83
	澳元	506.18	520.99	520.99	502.47	513.46	518.41
	新西兰元	482.84	495.69	497.38	480.98	490.88	486.14
	新加坡元	492.42	491.35	493.43	490.83	491.55	489.56
	瑞士法郎	703.74	708.88	708.88	697.45	702.64	691.17
	加元	504.86	521.44	521.44	502.95	510.93	514.88
	林吉特	62.852	63.376	63.376	62.666	62.847	63.730
	卢布	831.04	875.65	881.96	828.89	851.23	842.86

1979—2017年上半年人民币对美元交易中间价月平均汇价 ●
Monthly Average Transaction Mid Rates of Renminbi Against US dollar,1979—2016H1

人民币元/100美元
RMB per 100 USD

四、利用外资^①

Ⅳ. Foreign Investment Utilization

①资料来源：商务部。
Source: Ministry of Commerce.

2017年上半年利用外资

Foreign Direct Investment in the first half of 2017

利用外资方式 Mode of Foreign Investment Utilization	本年批准外资项目数 Approved Foreign Investment Programs		本年实际使用外资 Actual Utilization of Foreign Investment	
	本年累计 Accumulative in this Year	同比增长(%) Increase	本年累计 Accumulative in This Year	同比增长(%) Increase
总计 Total	15 053	12.3	656.5	−5.4
一、外商直接投资 Direct Foreign Investment	15 053	12.3	656.5	−5.4
中外合资企业 Sino−Foreign Equity Joint Venture	3 991	28.3	160.6	−11.0
中外合作企业 Sino−Foreign Contractual Joint Venture	51	−23.9	4.9	8.4
外资企业 Foreign Investment Enterprise	10 955	7.6	445.7	−3.1
外商投资股份制 Stock−Holding by Foreign Investment	56	36.6	45.2	−8.6
合作开发 Cooperation Exploitation	0	0.0	0	0.0
其他 Others	0	0.0	0	0.0
二、外商其他投资 Other Foreign Investment	0	0.0	0	0.0
对外发行股票 Issue Stocks to the Outside	0	0.0	0	0.0
国际租赁 International Tenancy	0	0.0	0	0.0
补偿贸易 Compensative Trade	0	0.0	0	0.0
加工装配 Processing & Assembling	0	0.0	0	0.0

注：统计数据为非金融领域。
Note: The data is subject to non−financial sectors.

五、外债①

V. External Debt

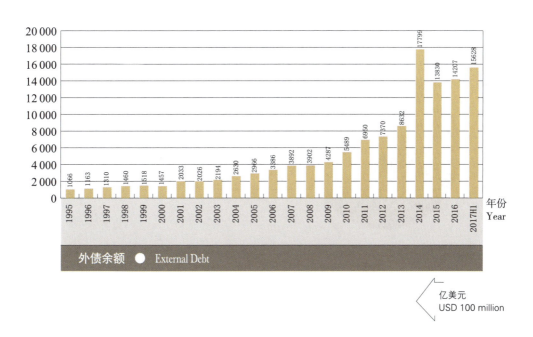

外债余额 ● External Debt

亿美元
USD 100 million

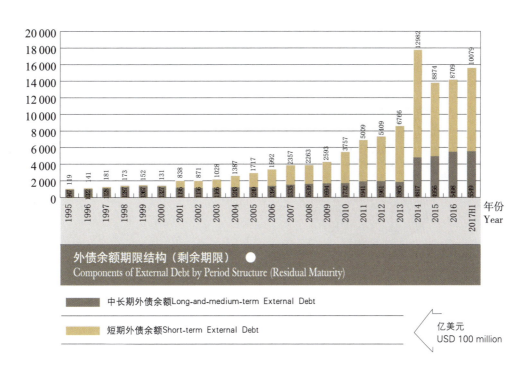

外债余额期限结构（剩余期限）●
Components of External Debt by Period Structure (Residual Maturity)

■ 中长期外债余额 Long-and-medium-term External Debt

■ 短期外债余额 Short-term External Debt

亿美元
USD 100 million

---

① 数据来源：国家外汇管理局。
Source: State Administration of Foreign Exchange.

2017上半年末外债余额期限结构（剩余期限）
Components of External Debt by Period Structure (Residual Maturity)，End—2017H1

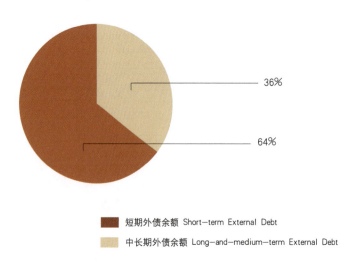

36%

64%

■ 短期外债余额 Short—term External Debt

■ 中长期外债余额 Long—and—medium—term External Debt

2017上半年末登记外债余额主体结构
Components of Registered External Debt by Type of Debtor，End—2017H1

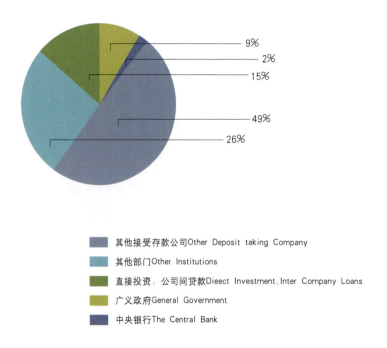

9%

2%

15%

49%

26%

■ 其他接受存款公司Other Deposit taking Company

■ 其他部门Other Institutions

■ 直接投资：公司间贷款Dieect Investment；Inter Company Loans

■ 广义政府General Government

■ 中央银行The Central Bank

六、世界经济增长状况①

VI. Growth of World Economics

世界主要经济体增长率 ● Growth Rate of Major Economies in the World

- ◆ - 中国 China   ....■.... 美国 USA   - ▲ - 欧元区 Euro Area   ● 日本 Japan

注：美国、日本和欧元区是实际GDP季比折年增速，中国为年比增速。
The growth rates of U.S, Japan and Euro Area are the annualized quarterly growth rates, and the growth rate of China is the year-on-year quarterly growth rate.

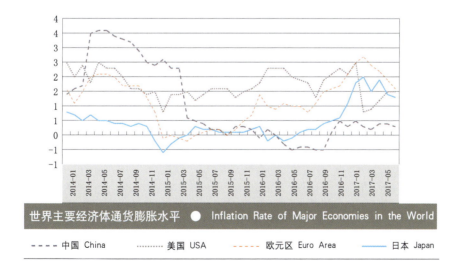

世界主要经济体通货膨胀水平 ● Inflation Rate of Major Economies in the World

- --- 中国 China   .... 美国 USA   - - - 欧元区 Euro Area   —— 日本 Japan

①资料来源：彭博资讯；CEIC Asia Database。
Sources: Bloomberg, CEIC Asia Database.

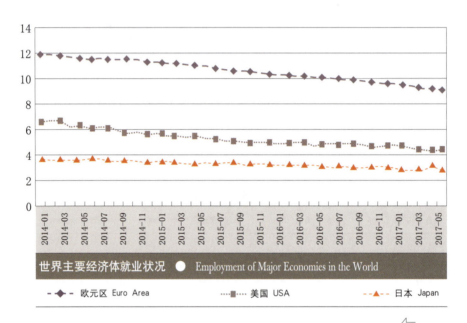

世界主要经济体就业状况 ● Employment of Major Economies in the World

- ◆ - 欧元区 Euro Area   ┈■┈ 美国 USA   - ▲ - 日本 Japan

失业率 (%)
Unemployment Rate (%)

七、国际金融市场状况^①

VII．International Financial Market

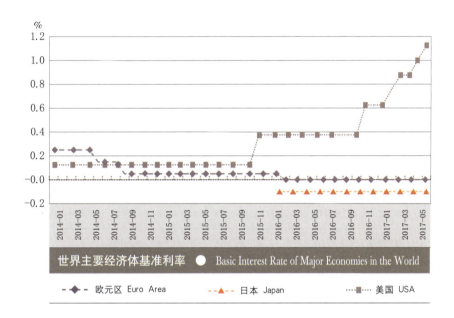

世界主要经济体基准利率 ● Basic Interest Rate of Major Economies in the World

- ◆ - 欧元区 Euro Area　　- ▲ - 日本 Japan　　······■······ 美国 USA

美国、德国及日本股票指数走势 ●
The trend of stock indices in the markets of USA, Germany and Japan

—— 道琼斯30种工业股票指数（左轴）Dow Jones Industrial 30 Average(LHS)

—— 日经225指数（左轴）Nikkei 225(LHS)

—— 法兰克福DAX指数（右轴）Frankfurt DAX(RHS)

①资料来源：彭博资讯。
Source: Bloomberg.

国际商品价格 ● Price of International Commodities

—— 高盛工业金属价格指数(总回报率)(左轴) Goldman Sachs Industrial Metal Index Total Return(LHS)

—— 纽约商品交易所原油期货价格（右轴） NYMEX Crude Oil Future Price(RHS)

美元/桶
USD/Barrel

伦敦金属交易所金银价格 ● LME Gold and Silver Price

—— 黄金（左轴）Gold(LHS)

—— 白银（右轴）Silver(RHS)

美元/盎司
USD/Ounce